THE QUICK SIX FIX

Asian Chicken and Mint Salad, page 37

THE QUICK SIX FIX

100 NO-FUSS, FULL-FLAVOR RECIPES

STUART O'KEEFFE

with Kathleen Squires

WILLIAM MORROW
An Imprint of HarperCollins*Publishers*

Crispy Salmon with Pistachio
Basil Butter, page 98

 For information address HarperCollins Publishers, 195 Broadway, New York, NY 10007.

HarperCollins books may be purchased for educational, business, or sales promotional use. For information please write: Special Markets Department, HarperCollins Publishers, 195 Broadway, New York, NY 10007.

FIRST EDITION

Design by Ashley Tucker
Photography by Joanne Murphy
Food styling by Sharon Hearne-Smith
Prop styling by Grace Campbell

Library of Congress Cataloging-in-Publication Data has been applied for.

ISBN 978-0-06-241975-0

16 17 18 19 20 OV/QGT 10 9 8 7 6 5 4 3 2 1

TO MY LATE AUNT DERRY,
for showing me how to bake amazing pastries and desserts. I truly miss your Guinness cake. Mine is never quite as good as yours was.

CONTENTS

Asian Burger, page 153

INTRODUCTION

There's an Irish proverb that best describes my approach to cooking: "There's no use boiling your cabbage twice." It actually has nothing to do with cooking; it's usually said when someone tends to revisit worries over and over. But if you take it more literally, it simply shows the folly in making too much of a fuss over anything—including cooking. I find that people tend to unnecessarily stress out over preparing a meal. It needn't be hard, and it doesn't have to require a lot of time. We're modern people living in modern times with all of the savvy, tools, and tricks to cook efficiently without sacrificing delicious results. Think about it: What good is a twice-boiled anything?

There's a reason for my affinity for Irish proverbs: I'm from Ireland, the small town Nenagh in County Tipperary, population just shy of eight thousand. Traditionally, it's a market town with one of Ireland's leading creameries. And we do love our cream and butter.

In my family, we were three boys and one girl, along with my parents. My mom always loved cooking and she never spared anything with food, even though we didn't have much money. Still, every Saturday she'd buy quality ingredients at the farmers' markets, including fresh meat, poultry, fruit, and vegetables along with all of that great dairy. And she cooked with great enjoyment—it was her hobby away from long hours working at her clothing store. By the age of seven, I had become her miniature sous-chef, helping to roll out dough for pastries, chopping vegetables for stew, and performing with glee any task she had given me. I relished the one-on-one time with her, not to mention the tasty treats she'd slip me in the process. When I wasn't cooking with my mom, I'd help my aunt, who was endlessly baking. She taught me how to achieve that perfectly flaky crust and a featherlight meringue. I'd assist her with everything from apple tarts to her Guinness cake to pavlova, still some of my favorite taste memories today.

Both my aunt and my mom didn't need a long list of ingredients. Nor did they use elaborate methods to prepare

good food. From them, the first inklings of my Quick Six Fix philosophy were born.

I went off to culinary school when I was nineteen, then cooked in kitchens in France, Dublin, and the Napa Valley. Those professional kitchens taught me how to respect my space, working efficiently while keeping it clean. Another component of the Quick Six Fix took hold then. I realized there's no reason why those ethics can't apply to the home kitchen, too.

Once I arrived in Los Angeles and I started to cook for parties and events, speed, efficiency, and flavor were always intertwined and became more essential. Celebrity clients relied on me for food that tasted great with a seemingly effortless approach (they certainly never wanted to walk into a dirty kitchen!). Cooking on television, on shows such as *Private Chefs of Beverly Hills* and *Stuart's Kitchen*, helped me streamline my kitchen, and methods, even more.

All of these influences, from my family to culinary school to cooking professionally to "playing" a chef on TV, all contributed to what I will share in this book. Once you get the hang of the Quick Six Fix philosophy, you'll never cook the same way again. You'll discover there's nothing half-baked here, with no cutting of corners. Nor, for that matter, is anything twice-boiled. The Quick Six Fix is simply an easy method yielding fully delicious food.

THE QUICK SIX FIX PHILOSOPHY

The Quick Six Fix is my approach to quick and easy, full-flavor cooking. It is designed to get you in and out of the kitchen fast so that you can take the time to enjoy your meal and your company. Each recipe in this book features no more than six minutes of prep, six minutes of cleanup, and six key ingredients. And most recipes are designed to be made in 30 minutes or less. The few that do require a little more time do not require any more effort—just a little more roasting in the oven to make that chicken perfect, for example, or a little more simmering to tenderize that stew.

THE KEYS TO THE QUICK SIX FIX

KEEP YOUR PANTRY STOCKED

Use "The Quick Six Fix Pantry" chapter as your perpetual shopping list. If you keep your pantry stocked with these go-to items, you'll always be prepared to make a quick, easy, tasty meal. Some of those items will figure into the "six ingredient" count, but note that a few essentials, like salt and olive oil, don't factor into the count. (The six ingredients that amount to the count are denoted by bold text, while the essentials are in regular type.) The bottom line is that a well-stocked pantry also allows for more efficient grocery shopping.

FRESH IS BEST

When shopping for groceries, keep in mind that fresh is best, whether you're buying fish, pasta, vegetables, or even herbs. Freshness makes all the difference in terms of flavor.

DON'T SWEAT THE PREP

You know the maxim "forewarned is forearmed"? Remember it when using this book. I can't stress how important this is (and in fact, I will annoyingly remind you of it throughout the book): Before starting a recipe, read the recipe through several times! Three times should be the charm so that you have a good understanding of what's needed, what's going to happen, and how you can best manage your time. It's also a great idea to quickly read the text at the beginning of the chapter of the recipe to brush up on general tips and tools. Once you have a grasp of what's to happen, there will be no surprises, and you'll breeze through the prep. By my Quick Six Fix definition, prep means anything that requires labor—chopping, peeling, and grating, for example. Measuring and boiling water are not considered prep, in my book. Prep times are listed at the beginning of each recipe.

WHAT YOU'LL NEED

The tools you'll need for my recipes are pretty basic. Nevertheless, I have listed those required at the beginning of each chapter. So again, it's a good idea to browse the beginning of the section before you begin to cook.

THE SECRET TO CLEANUP SUCCESS

I use something called a Reverse Traffic Light Theory for efficient cleanup. This is cribbed from a trick I learned in culinary school. Throughout certain recipes, you'll notice this traffic light icon . Usually you'll see this once you've put a casserole dish in the oven or left a pan on simmer or are waiting for pasta to boil. What that means is STOP! Take just a few minutes to YIELD to any mess you've made. This is the time to wipe the cutting board, soak a pan, stick the bowls in the dishwasher, and use your time efficiently before you GO back to cooking. You'll be surprised at how just being reminded to assess your mess will help in the end. When you have your feet up instead of lingering in the kitchen with the dirty dishes, you will thank me!

The methods in my recipes are also designed for quicker cleanup. Tricks like lining a baking pan with foil, using a Ziploc bag for marinades, and cooking one-pot meals are all huge time-savers.

Cleanup times are listed at the beginning of the recipe.

KEEP IN MIND: I'M A GOOD TIPPER

There are helpful tips throughout the book—at the beginning of each section, in the headnotes, and within the recipes themselves. Pay attention to them, from folding parchment paper to properly cutting meat; they are all designed to make your cooking easier and better.

MIX AND MATCH

Each main comes with suggested side dishes, but feel free to experiment and mix and match your own meals to your liking. Just pick a salad and a dessert and you've got the makings of an easy feast!

ENJOY!

The most important part of making a meal is enjoying the process and the results. So let's get started! Six ingredients; six minutes of prep; six minutes of cleanup; over 100 no-fuss, full-flavor recipes.

RECIPE KEY

These icons are designed to give you the quick 411 on recipes throughout:

 indicates a dish that uses one pot, one baking sheet, or one skillet—only one cooking vessel to clean!

indicates a vegetarian dish.

indicates that the recipe makes a complete meal.

 is my gentle attempt at haranguing you into reading through a recipe before you start.

 And of course, don't forget what the Traffic Light means: STOP! YIELD to your mess. And GO back to cooking.

Ingredients in black type are your pantry staples; they do not count as one of the six ingredients (or fewer) that you need to shop for.

Ingredients in **BOLD CAPS** are among the six ingredients (or fewer) you need to put on your shopping list especially for that recipe.

THE QUICK SIX FIX PANTRY

Use this as your shopping list for this cookbook. Keeping these items on hand will ensure that you can make a Quick Six Fix meal at a moment's notice.

MUST HAVE

- **Baking powder**
- **Baking soda**
- **Beans** (canned)
  - **Black beans**
  - **Cannellini beans**
- **Bread**
- **Butter** (I like unsalted Kerry Gold)
- **Cheese**
  - **Parmesan**
- **Chocolate** (semisweet, 60% cacao)
- **Cocoa powder**
- **Coconut milk**
- **Eggs**
- **Flour** (all-purpose)
- **Garlic** (fresh and jarred)
- **Heavy cream**
- **Hoisin sauce**
- **Lemon**
- **Lime**
- **Mayonnaise**
- **Milk**
- **Mustard** (Dijon)
- **Oils**
  - **Canola oil**
  - **Extra virgin olive oil**
- **Onions**
- **Pasta** (always three types)
  - **Angel hair or capellini**
  - **Elbow macaroni**
  - **Spaghetti**
- **Peas** (frozen)
- **Rice**
  - **Long grain**
- **Sesame seeds**
- **Soy sauce** (low sodium)
- **Spices**
  - **Black pepper** (fresh ground)
  - **Dried chili flakes** (aka red pepper flakes)
  - **Cinnamon** (ground)
  - **Garlic powder**
  - **Old Bay seasoning**
  - **Onion powder**
  - **Paprika**
  - **Salt** (kosher)
- **Stocks** (low sodium and concentrated)
  - **Beef**
  - **Chicken**
  - **Vegetable**
- **Sugar**
  - **Brown**
  - **White** (granulated)
  - **White** (superfine)
- **Tomatoes** (28-ounce can, San Marzano, diced)
- **Tomato paste**
- **Vanilla extract**
- **Vinegar**
  - **Balsamic**
  - **Cider**
  - **Rice wine**
  - **White**
- **Wine**
  - **Red** (cabernet, port)
  - **White** (chardonnay)

NICE TO HAVE

- Artichokes (jarred or canned)
- **Capers**
- **Chili garlic paste**
- **Coffee** (dark roast)
- **Fish sauce**
- **Herbs**
  - **Oregano** (dried)
  - **Parsley** (fresh and dried)
  - **Thyme** (dried)
- **Hot sauce**
- **Jam**
- **Ketchup**
- **Maple syrup**
- **Nuts**
  - **Almonds**
  - **Pecans**
  - **Walnuts**
- **Nutella**
- **Oats** (old fashioned)
- **Olives** (green, jarred)
- **Oils**
  - **Coconut**
  - **Peanut**
  - **Sesame**
- **Pasta**
  - **Fettuccine**
  - **Linguine**
  - **Bucatini**
- **Polenta**
- **Spices**
  - **Cayenne pepper**
  - **Chili powder**
  - **Cumin**
  - **Peppercorns** (black whole)
  - **Sea salt**
- **Spirits**
  - **Brandy**
  - **Whiskey**
- **Sriracha**
- **Sun-dried tomatoes**
- **Udon noodles**

Tip: Baking goods like flour and sugar stay a lot fresher in air-tight canisters and also keep your pantry looking a lot more organized.

Open-Faced Tortilla
Breakfast, page 9

BREAK-FAST

Breakfast is my favorite meal, not to mention the most essential meal of the day. If I somehow miss breakfast, I end up cranky all day. That's not a good thing—no one wants to be around me when I'm cranky. One thing that puts a smile on my face is a breakfast that is creative, reasonably healthy, and fast and easy to make. Not sold yet? Here are a few reasons why breakfast (or brekkie, as we call it in Ireland) is so important:

- Morning is when your body needs nutrients most. Feed your body and you'll be set energy-wise for the day.
- If you skip breakfast, you're likely to overeat later in the day and make some poor dietary choices.
- A well-nourished body allows the mind to focus well. You have to admit it's great to start the day with a tightly tuned brain.

The following breakfasts show the variety you can enjoy for a morning meal, while using only three or four ingredients. These can literally be made and served in under 15 minutes.

Tools

Baking sheet (13" x 9")
Blender
Butter knife
Bowls of various sizes
Chef's knife
Cutting board
Fork
Measuring spoons
Measuring cups
Saucepan (large, 4-quart)
Skillets (10-inch, 12-inch, nonstick)
Slotted spoon
Spatula
Spoon
Toaster
Tongs
Whisk

3x
Don't forget! Read through a recipe 3 TIMES before you begin!

OPEN-FACED TORTILLA BREAKFAST

Serves 4

PREP 2 minutes
COOK 10 minutes
CLEAN 5 minutes

This is a morning favorite, with a bit of a Latin spin. The tortilla base makes a great crispy bed for the eggs. But the best part of this dish is you can make the cumin and sour cream ahead, stash it in the fridge, and serve this up even more quickly.

- Canola oil (enough to cover 1 inch of pan)
- 4 **CORN TORTILLAS**
- ½ cup **SOUR CREAM**
- 1 teaspoon hot sauce, plus extra to serve if desired
- 1 teaspoon ground cumin
- 1 teaspoon kosher salt
- 12 medium eggs, beaten
- 2 tablespoons crumbled **FETA CHEESE**
- 1 tablespoon fresh **CILANTRO LEAVES**

Let's Do Breakfast!

1. In a large nonstick skillet over medium-high heat, heat 1 inch canola oil and lightly crisp the corn tortillas, about 30 seconds per side. Set aside on a plate lined with paper towels and repeat.

2. In a bowl, combine sour cream, hot sauce, cumin, and salt. Mix well and set aside.

3. Reduce heat to medium. Drain off all but ½ tablespoon of the oil in the pan and add the beaten eggs. Stir, scraping the bottom of the pan with a heatproof spatula so that the eggs don't burn or stick, until cooked and scrambled, about 3 to 4 minutes.

4. Divide corn tortillas among 4 plates. Top with cooked eggs.

5. Top with a dollop of sour cream mixture and sprinkle with feta cheese and cilantro.

6. Serve with hot sauce.

LEMON CHILI AVOCADO TOAST

Serves 4
PREP 5 minutes
COOK 5 minutes
CLEAN 2 minutes

In California, we always have access to great avocados. And when life gives you an abundance of avocados, you make avocado toast, of course! There are several varieties of avocado, and any of them would work for this recipe. However, I prefer using the Hass variety—the small type with the dark, bumpy skin—as they have more natural fat and are less watery than the larger, smooth-skinned sort. Hass avocados add a wonderfully smooth, creamy texture. The lemon and chili act as the perfect eye-openers.

2 ripe **AVOCADOS**, halved and pitted
Juice of 1 lemon
½ teaspoon sea salt
½ teaspoon freshly ground pepper
4 slices **WHOLE WHEAT BREAD**
1 teaspoon dried chili flakes

Let's Do Breakfast!

1. Scoop the flesh out of the avocado shells and place in a bowl.
2. Add lemon juice and salt and pepper. Mash well with a fork. Set aside.
3. Toast bread and spread each slice with avocado mixture.
4. Sprinkle with chili flakes and serve.

Tip: To pit an avocado, take a sharp knife and slice the avocado lengthwise, cutting around the pit. Once you've gone the circumference, twist the top half off the bottom. Then take a chef's knife and swiftly "chop" the pit until the blade sticks into it. Then twist the blade to remove the pit from the avocado.

SPEEDY GONZALES EGGS

Serves 4
PREP 6 minutes
COOK 10 minutes
CLEAN 5 minutes

In LA, no matter where you go for breakfast, there is always some version of Mexican-style eggs, whether they are spiked with hot sauce, smothered with tomatillo salsa, or served with fried tortilla strips. This is my version of south-of-the-border eggs. The chili flakes are a great way to jazz up the usual eggs on toast.

- 2 tablespoons canola oil
- ¾ cup **CHERRY TOMATOES**, halved
- ½ teaspoon dried chili flakes
- 8 medium eggs, beaten
- 1 teaspoon kosher salt
- 1 teaspoon freshly cracked pepper
- 2 **GREEN ONIONS**, roughly chopped, divided
- 1 cup crushed **TORTILLA CHIPS**
- 4 slices **SOURDOUGH BREAD**, toasted
- Unsalted butter for spreading

Let's Do Breakfast!

1. Heat 2 tablespoons canola oil in a skillet over medium heat. Add tomatoes and chili flakes and cook for 2 minutes.

2. In a bowl, season beaten eggs with salt and pepper. Add to hot skillet.

3. Cook eggs, scraping the bottom of the pan with a heatproof spatula so eggs do not stick and burn, about 3 to 5 minutes.

4. Add one green onion and cook for about 1 minute until eggs are yellow and fluffy.

5. Add crushed tortilla chips to the eggs and quickly stir.

6. Divide eggs onto 4 plates and sprinkle with extra green onion. Serve with buttered toast.

☆ Cleaning Tip: To remove stubborn egg sticking to the pan, pour some white vinegar in the pan and bring it to a simmer. The egg will run right off.

POACHED EGGS, GOAT CHEESE, AND SPINACH on Toast

Serves 4

PREP 3 minutes

COOK 25 minutes

CLEAN 6 minutes

I know that you're intimidated by the thought of poaching eggs. If you do it wrong, it can make an inedible mess. But do it correctly and you've got heaven. I share my tips for attaining heaven at right.

The flavor in this dish brings me back to France 2002, during my culinary arts years in college. My friend Simon and I would rummage through the restaurant to make breakfast. Together we came up with this creamy masterpiece.

1 tablespoon distilled white vinegar

4 tablespoons unsalted butter (divided)

6 cups **SPINACH** leaves

½ teaspoon kosher salt

½ teaspoon freshly ground black pepper

4 medium eggs

4 slices **WHOLE WHEAT BREAD** (country style is best)

4 ounces **GOAT CHEESE**

Extra virgin olive oil for garnish

Let's Do Breakfast!

1. In a large saucepan, bring 3 inches of water to a simmer. Add vinegar.

2. Meanwhile, heat 2 tablespoons butter in a large nonstick skillet over medium-high heat. Add 3 cups spinach leaves and cook until softened, about 3 to 4 minutes. Repeat with the remaining butter and spinach. Season with salt and pepper and set aside, covered.

3. Crack one egg at a time in a small bowl and slide the egg gently into the simmering water. Cook until the egg whites are opaque (about 30 seconds) before adding the next egg. (Be patient and take your time. It may take a few tries to get it right, but when you do, it's impressive.) Continue cooking for about 3 to 4 minutes. Using a slotted spoon, remove the eggs onto a plate lined with paper towels.

4. Toast the bread. Spread the slices with goat cheese and place on four plates. Top with spinach and one egg per slice of toast.

5. Drizzle with some extra virgin olive oil and a light sprinkle of salt. Serve.

Tips on poaching an egg:

1. Always use fresh eggs; they hold together better.
2. Make sure the water is at a simmer—not too cold and not at a rolling boil.
3. Carefully lift the eggs from the bottom with your slotted spoon.

A MANHATTAN BREAKFAST

Serves 4

PREP 6 minutes

COOK 6 minutes

CLEAN 3 minutes

When I was on my first trip to New York City, this sandwich made as much of an impression on me as the towering skyscrapers. It was the first thing I ate in the Big Apple. I arrived at my hotel early in the morning and picked up something like this in a nearby deli. It was a completely satisfying eggless sandwich, piled with salmon, tomato, cucumber, onion, and cream cheese. I remember it steeled me for the hectic pace of a city day.

- 4 slices **PUMPERNICKEL BREAD** (8 if they are small)
- 4 tablespoons **CREAM CHEESE**, at room temperature
- 1 **TOMATO**, sliced
- 8 thin slices **CUCUMBER**, julienned
- 8 ounces **SMOKED SALMON**
- ½ **RED ONION**, diced
- Pinch sea salt (Maldon is great)

Let's Do Breakfast!

1. Toast pumpernickel bread.

2. Spread with cream cheese and top with (in the following order): tomato, cucumber, smoked salmon, and onion. Repeat with all slices.

3. Sprinkle each with a pinch of sea salt and serve.

GOAT CHEESE SCRAMBLE

Serves 4
PREP 5 minutes
COOK 15 minutes
CLEAN 3 minutes

Everyone has a favorite style of cooking for eggs. My particular favorite is scrambled. I love that they are fluffy and easy to make and that you can pretty much add anything you want to them. Goat cheese brings a tart flavor and creamy texture to this scramble, while the additions of diced bacon and tomato make for a full breakfast in each light, feathery forkful.

- 2 teaspoons unsalted butter, plus more for toast
- 2 teaspoons canola oil
- 4 slices **BACON**, diced
- ½ **RED ONION**, diced
- 12 medium eggs, beaten
- 4 ounces **GOAT CHEESE** or **CREAM CHEESE**
- 1 cup **CHERRY TOMATOES**, halved
- 1 teaspoon chopped **CHIVES**
- 4 slices toasted **SOURDOUGH BREAD**

Let's Do Breakfast!

1. In a large nonstick skillet over medium heat, heat butter and oil together.

2. Add bacon and cook for about 4 to 6 minutes. Then add onion and cook for 2 more minutes.

3. Add eggs and cook, stirring with a heatproof spatula until all ingredients are scrambled and cooked to your liking, about 5 to 7 minutes.

4. Stir in goat cheese and continue cooking for one minute. Divide on plates. Top with tomatoes and chives. Enjoy with the buttered toasted sourdough bread.

FYI: Adding canola oil to butter helps prevent the butter from burning.

BLUEBERRY KICK SMOOTHIE

Serves 4

PREP 1 minute

COMBINING 1 minute

CLEAN 1 minute

When I am pressed for time in the morning, this is the most filling, fast, and easy breakfast I can make. And I can take it on the go and drink it on the way. The key is always having these ingredients on hand. My secret: adding oatmeal to smoothies. It makes it more like a meal, less like a drink. This makes a great afternoon snack, too.

- 2 cups whole milk
- 2 cups **GREEK YOGURT** (vanilla or plain)
- 2 cups **FROZEN BLUEBERRIES**
- 1 cup **INSTANT OATMEAL**
- 4 teaspoons **HONEY**
- 2 cups ice

Let's Do Breakfast!

1. Place all ingredients in a blender and process until smooth.
2. Pour into 4 glasses and top with extra blueberries.

Tip: This smoothie can be made with any fruit. Sub in your favorite!

CHOCOLATE PEANUT BUTTER SUNDAE SMOOTHIE

Serves 4

PREP 2 minutes

COMBINING 1 minute

CLEAN 1 minute

Though I prefer this yummy drink as a midafternoon snack, it makes a lovely breakfast smoothie, too. You've got the potassium from the bananas to get you going; the protein of the peanut butter for lasting energy; plus the pep of chocolate, along with the slight guilty pleasure of having it in the morning.

2 frozen peeled **BANANAS**

2 cups milk

2 cups whole milk **GREEK YOGURT** (vanilla or plain)

4 tablespoons **SMOOTH PEANUT BUTTER**

4 tablespoons **CHOCOLATE SYRUP**

Let's Do Breakfast!

1. Place all ingredients in a blender and process until smooth.
2. Pour into 4 glasses and drizzle with some extra syrup.

Tip: If you buy a bunch of bananas and it looks like they might go bad before you eat them all, peel them, put them in a Ziploc baggie, and toss them in the freezer. They are great to have on hand for making smoothies or banana bread, and are a great guilt-free snack on their own, like a Popsicle!

Tip: For a healthier option, use nonfat milk and nonfat yogurt.

SCHOOL-MORNING OATMEAL

Serves 4
PREP 2 minutes
COOK 8 minutes
CLEAN 5 minutes

When I was growing up in Ireland, my dad would wake up at seven a.m. each morning to make us all porridge before we went off to school. He swore by it as a breakfast that keeps you full for a long time. Dad's porridge was fine; he made it with water. But I really looked forward to those mornings when Mom would make it because she used cream and milk and served it with jam from the local farmers' market. Obviously, Mom's was richer and tastier. Sorry, Dad.

¾ cup sliced **ALMONDS**
4 cups whole milk
¾ cup heavy cream
1 teaspoon **ALMOND EXTRACT**
3 tablespoons sugar
1 teaspoon kosher salt
3 cups **OLD-FASHIONED OATS** (Quaker is good)
4 tablespoons **STRAWBERRY JAM**

Let's Do Breakfast!

1. Preheat oven to 350°F. Spread almonds on a baking sheet and place in the oven for 5 to 7 minutes. Toss halfway through baking and keep a close eye on them so they do not burn. Set aside.

2. Meanwhile, combine milk, cream, almond extract, sugar, and salt in a large saucepan.

3. Bring to a boil, add oats, reduce the heat, and simmer for 5 minutes.

STOP! WHILE OATMEAL IS SIMMERING, CLEAN BAKING SHEET.

4. Serve porridge in bowls. Top each with a tablespoon of jam and sprinkle with toasted almonds.

Tip: You can use all milk instead of the milk/cream mixture, or sub in some almond milk for an extra nutty flavor. Don't have almond extract on hand? Vanilla extract works just as well.

Tip: Keep an eye on the almonds while they are toasting, as they tend to burn quickly.

SALADS

Kale, Fingerling Potato, and Bacon Salad, page 45

I love a good, hearty salad. I'm not talking about a few leaves scattered in a bowl and dressed. I'm talking about something that provides a great amount of nutrition and can very well fill me up on a night that I feel like eating somewhat lighter . . . but not necessarily light. Salads are also a great way to use your leftovers. Those potatoes you have lingering in your fridge from the day before? That extra steak? The half a rotisserie chicken you didn't finish? Toss them all in! You can mix and match my collection of salads with any of my Quick Six Dressing recipes—I make a few suggestions with each for great flavor pairings.

QUICK SIX SALAD TIPS

- To properly dress a salad: Use a stainless steel bowl and dress the sides of the bowl with the dressing; then, using your hands, toss the greens around.
- Many of these salads can easily become vegetarian, and are just as tasty, by eliminating the meat.
- It's a good idea to buy fresh greens in a bag or package to save time on washing.
- A cooked rotisserie chicken is your friend and secret weapon! Make any salad more substantial by adding the meat, shredded from a premade chicken. One 2-pound chicken will give you 3 cups of meat off the bone—2 cups white and 1 cup dark. Keep leftover chicken in a sealed container or Ziploc bag in the fridge for up to four days.

QUICK SIX DRESSING TIPS

- When making your own vinaigrettes, stick to a 3-to-1 ratio—3 parts oil to 1 part vinegar. When making more or less, scale up or down accordingly.
- Always add olive oil in a slow stream so that it emulsifies properly.
- All of my dressings will keep up to 5 days in the refrigerator in an airtight container, preferably glass.

A GUIDE TO THE OILS YOU WILL USE IN THIS BOOK

CANOLA • Canola oil has a high smoke point and is great for frying. It's also good for baking and salad dressing.

COCONUT • Great for baking and for imparting a tropical flair in cooked dishes.

OLIVE • Olive oil comes in various grades of refinement. Extra virgin is the most refined and the most expensive. Save the costly stuff for garnish. Use lesser grades for sautéing and dressings.

PEANUT • Wonderful earthy flavor and great for frying!

SESAME • Another super fragrant, super flavorful oil. It's perfect for adding an Asian flavor.

Tools

Aluminum foil

Baking sheet (rimmed, 18" x 13" and 26" x 18")

Blender or food processor

Bowls (of various sizes, including one of heatproof glass)

Chef's knife

Cutting board

Glass jar

Paper towels

Skillets (10-inch and 12-inch, cast-iron, or grill pans of equal size)

Spatula

Saucepan (small)

Tongs

Whisk

Ziploc bags

A GUIDE TO VINEGARS YOU WILL USE IN THIS BOOK

BALSAMIC • This vinegar has a distinct dark brown color and sometimes a syrupy texture. Its slightly sweet flavor allows great versatility—balsamic is great in everything from salad dressings to desserts.

CIDER • Made from apples, this vinegar is great for imparting a clean, fruity flavor in marinades.

RED WINE • The sharp flavor of this vinegar makes for a great marinade and is also a go-to for salad dressings.

RICE WINE • This is a must to lend Asian flavors to salads and stir-frys.

SHERRY • Made from fortified wine, sherry vinegar makes a spectacular addition to sauces.

WHITE (DISTILLED) • This very strong vinegar can be used in salad dressings and for pickling. Its power also makes it great for cleaning.

WHITE WINE • Not as sharp as red wine vinegar, the white wine variety is another salad dressing go-to.

Remember the power of reading through a recipe 3 TIMES!

Tip: For storing dressing, I consider a mason jar the ultimate choice. It has a good seal, which makes it easy to shake and emulsify for use.

LIME AVOCADO DRESSING

Makes 1 cup
PREP 3 minutes
COMBINING 1 minute
CLEAN 2 minutes

This is the creamiest, most refreshing dressing you will ever enjoy, ever. If you keep a jar in your fridge, as I do, know that the lime will keep it from turning brown.

1 ripe **AVOCADO**, peeled, pit removed
¾ cup **SOUR CREAM**
Juice of 1 lime
2 cloves garlic, peeled
1 teaspoon kosher salt
1 teaspoon freshly ground black pepper

Let's Mix!

1. Place all ingredients in a food processor or blender and process until well mixed and creamy.

2. Store in an airtight container and refrigerate up to 5 days.

Tip: When citrus is called for in a dressing, always use fresh-squeezed juice, not canned, cartoned, or frozen. It makes a tremendous difference in flavor!

STU'S SUPER CITRUS VINAIGRETTE

Makes 1 cup
PREP 6 minutes
COMBINING 3 minutes
CLEAN 5 minutes

This is light and tangy—a great go-to dressing when I crave a citrus punch on my greens.

Juice of 1 medium **ORANGE**
Zest of ½ **ORANGE**
Juice of 2 limes (about ½ cup)
Juice of 1 lemon
Zest of 1 lemon
1 tablespoon balsamic vinegar
1 large **SHALLOT**, minced
¼ teaspoon dried chili flakes
½ teaspoon kosher salt
½ teaspoon freshly ground black pepper
1 teaspoon Dijon mustard
¼ cup extra virgin olive oil

Let's Mix!

1. Combine all ingredients except the olive oil in a glass bowl and whisk.

2. While whisking, slowly add the extra virgin olive oil in a stream to the ingredients until emulsified.

3. Store in an airtight container and refrigerate up to 5 days.

Tip: A simple way to juice citrus is to roll it on the counter first to release juice from the segments; then cut it in half and pierce it with a fork. Use the hand not holding the fork to twist and release juice. Zest the citrus first and then slice in half to juice.

BALSAMIC DRESSING

Makes 1 cup

PREP 2 minutes
COMBINING 2 minutes
CLEAN 2 minutes

If you have been using my Quick Six Fix Pantry as your shopping list, then the best thing about this dressing is that you will have all of these ingredients on hand at all times. This is a classic vinaigrette that every home cook should know how to make.

- 4 tablespoons balsamic vinegar
- 2 tablespoons water
- 1½ teaspoons Dijon mustard
- 1 clove garlic, minced
- ½ teaspoon kosher salt
- ½ teaspoon freshly ground black pepper
- ½ cup extra virgin olive oil

Let's Mix!

1. Whisk vinegar, water, mustard, garlic, salt, and pepper in a glass bowl.
2. Whisking continuously, slowly add the olive oil in a stream to the rest of the ingredients until emulsified.
3. Store in an airtight container and refrigerate up to 5 days.

ASIAN DRESSING FROM UP THE STREET

Makes 1 cup

PREP 5 minutes
COMBINING 3 minutes
CLEAN 3 minutes

There is a great Chinese restaurant that I frequent around the corner from where I live in Los Angeles. I always order this sesame ginger chicken salad there because I just adore the dressing that comes with it. The waiter can give me only so much information regarding the "secret" recipe, so this is my best attempt at re-creating it and its perky, nutty flavor. I have to say, this recipe comes pretty darn close!

- 2 teaspoons grated **FRESH GINGER**
- 2 cloves garlic, minced
- 1½ teaspoons rice wine vinegar
- 2 teaspoons superfine white sugar
- 3 tablespoons soy sauce
- ⅓ cup peanut oil or canola oil
- 1½ tablespoons toasted **SESAME OIL**
- 1 tablespoon chopped **FRESH CHIVES**
- 2 teaspoons toasted sesame seeds

Let's Mix!

1. Whisk together the ginger, garlic, rice wine vinegar, sugar, and soy sauce in a glass bowl.

2. Whisking continuously, add the peanut oil (or canola oil), then the sesame oil, each in a slow stream, until well combined.

3. Stir in the chives and sesame seeds.

4. Store in an airtight container and refrigerate up to 5 days.

Tip: If you can't find toasted sesame seeds, buy regular white sesame seeds and toast them in a dry skillet over medium heat for a minute or two.

MUSTARD HERB DRESSING

Makes 1 cup

PREP 4 minutes
COMBINING 2 minutes
CLEAN 3 minutes

I'll confess: I'm not a big fan of mustard. There's something about the heat that gets into my nasal passages. But this recipe uses just the perfect hint, playing up all the good qualities of the condiment. Plus, the herbs help balance the sharpness here.

3 cloves garlic, minced
4 tablespoons balsamic vinegar
2 teaspoons Dijon mustard
¾ cup extra virgin olive oil
½ teaspoon dried **PARSLEY**
½ teaspoon dried **THYME**
½ teaspoon kosher salt
½ teaspoon freshly ground black pepper

Let's Mix!

1. Whisk together the garlic, vinegar, and mustard until well combined.
2. Whisking continuously, add the olive oil in a slow stream until emulsified.
3. Stir in the parsley, thyme, salt, and pepper.
4. Store in an airtight container and refrigerate up to 5 days.

BUTTERMILK DRESSING

Makes 1 cup

PREP 2 minutes
COMBINING 1 minute
CLEAN 2 minutes

Ever since I came to the United States, I've been obsessed with buttermilk dressing. It just seems so . . . American. It's versatile and it goes with pretty much any salad you can think of. And it makes a great dip for fresh vegetables!

- ½ cup **BUTTERMILK**
- ½ cup mayonnaise
- Juice of 1 lemon
- 1½ tablespoons minced fresh **CHIVES**
- 1½ tablespoons chopped fresh **PARSLEY**
- ½ teaspoon kosher salt
- ½ teaspoon freshly ground black pepper

Let's Mix!

1. Whisk together all ingredients until well combined.
2. Store in an airtight container and refrigerate up to 5 days.

STEAKHOUSE SALAD

Serves 4
PREP 6 minutes
COOK 20 minutes
CLEAN 5 minutes

We all should have a good steak salad in our back pocket. First of all, it's a great use of leftovers. And in the warm weather, when you crave protein, it's a nice cool way to eat meat without serving it hot.

FOR THE STEAK MARINADE:

¼ cup balsamic vinegar
¼ cup low sodium soy sauce
¼ cup port wine
1 teaspoon dried chili flakes

FOR THE SALAD:

1 pound **SKIRT STEAK** or **FLANK STEAK**, trimmed of fat, sinew, and membrane
2 cups **CHERRY TOMATOES**, halved
½ **RED ONION**, thinly sliced
¾ cup **BLUE CHEESE** crumbles
3 tablespoons balsamic vinegar
1 tablespoon extra virgin olive oil
½ teaspoon kosher salt
½ teaspoon freshly ground black pepper
¾ pound **ARUGULA**

Let's Toss!

1. Combine all marinade ingredients in a Ziploc bag. Add steak and set aside for about 10 minutes.

2. In a large glass bowl, add cherry tomatoes, red onion, blue cheese, balsamic vinegar, extra virgin olive oil, salt, and pepper. Stir until all ingredients are well coated.

3. Remove steak from bag and set aside.

4. Light a grill or bring a cast-iron skillet to a medium-high heat. Cook the steak on each side for about 3 minutes. Set aside on a plate and let rest under tented aluminum foil for about 5 minutes.

STOP! WASH BOWLS.

5. Slice steak into ¼-inch slices. (See tips for slicing steak, p. 146.)

6. On 4 plates, evenly distribute arugula leaves and top with sliced steak. Spoon tomato salad on top of steak and serve.

★ Tip: Save time and have the butcher trim your meat.

FYI: One 2-pound rotisserie chicken will yield 3 cups of meat: 2 cups white and 1 cup dark.

ASIAN CHICKEN AND MINT SALAD

Serves 4
PREP 6 minutes
COOK 10 minutes
CLEAN 5 minutes

This is a lovely, simple, clean-tasting assembly of Asian ingredients—and something I could very likely eat every night. Because of its simple freshness and the lightness of the mint, this salad can make you feel downright saintly while you are eating it. I like to change it up sometimes by substituting grilled steak for the chicken and rice noodles for the cabbage. Try it!

- ½ cup Asian Dressing from up the Street (page 32)
- 2 **GREEN ONIONS** (scallions), roughly chopped
- 1 head **WHITE CABBAGE**, shredded or roughly chopped
- 1 large **CARROT**, washed, peeled, and grated
- 1 two-pound **ROTISSERIE CHICKEN**, shredded (about 3 cups)
- 10–15 **MINT** leaves, torn
- 10–15 **CILANTRO** leaves
- Salt to taste
- Freshly ground black pepper to taste
- ½ teaspoon sesame seeds

Let's Toss!

1. In a large bowl, thoroughly mix half the dressing with the green onion and cabbage and set aside (this helps soften the cabbage before serving).

2. In another large bowl, toss the rest of the dressing with the carrot, chicken, mint, and cilantro until combined.

3. Season, if needed, with salt and pepper to taste.

4. Divide cabbage salad between four plates, top with the chicken mixture, and serve. Garnish with some sesame seeds.

Tip: Save prep time by purchasing cabbage that is already shredded.

HAIL KALE BUTTERMILK CHICKEN SALAD

Serves 4
PREP 6 minutes
COOK 12 minutes
CLEAN 5 minutes

Yes, kale is trendy—it's everywhere! So why not make good use of its availability? I have really gotten into it lately. Kale is packed with nutrients and is high in fiber, low in fat, and super rich in iron and vitamin K. I love its green, earthy, fresh flavor. The chicken in this salad gives the dish a satisfying protein punch while the sourdough fills the tummy. That's exactly what you want in a salad, right?

5 tablespoons Buttermilk Dressing (page 34)

½ teaspoon kosher salt

½ teaspoon freshly ground black pepper

½ pound **KALE**, stems discarded, leaves roughly chopped

1 two-pound **ROTISSERIE CHICKEN**, meat removed (about 3 cups)

2 tablespoons olive oil

3 slices thick **COUNTRY WHITE** or **SOURDOUGH BREAD**, cut into ½-inch cubes

⅓ cup dried **CRANBERRIES**

¼ cup sliced **ALMONDS**

½ cup grated Parmesan cheese

Let's Toss!

1. In a large bowl, toss dressing, salt, and pepper with the kale and chicken until well coated. Divide among 4 plates and set aside.

2. Heat olive oil in a nonstick skillet set over medium heat. Add the cubed bread. Cook, stirring, until the cubes begin to brown up and become crisp. This should take about 5 to 7 minutes. Remove from the pan with a slotted spoon to be placed on the salad.

3. Sprinkle croutons, cranberries, almonds, and Parmesan cheese on top of each salad. Serve.

☆ Tip: The texture of kale can be tough. Dressing the leaves beforehand while you cook the bread will soften it before serving. Giving those leaves a good massage with your hands will make them even softer.

Tip: Use leftover chicken for this recipe, or simply purchase a cooked one from the supermarket, break it apart, and use the meat. Leftover chicken can be placed in a resealable bag and kept in the fridge for up to 4 days.

Tip: Save time and ask your butcher to trim your skirt steak

BLTA STEAK SALAD

Serves 4
PREP 6 minutes
COOK 20 minutes
CLEAN 5 minutes

I love a great BLTA—bacon, lettuce, tomato, avocado—sandwich. Why can't those same fresh, salty, creamy flavors mingle together in a salad? The addition of the A especially makes this a Los Angeles staple. California grows fantastic avocados, and they are available pretty much year-round. They bring the "A" game to this salad while adding a bit of creaminess.

- 1 pound **SKIRT STEAK**, trimmed of fat, sinew, and membrane
- 1 teaspoon kosher salt
- 1 teaspoon freshly ground black pepper
- 1 tablespoon canola oil
- 4 tablespoons Mustard Herb (page 33), Balsamic (page 31), or Buttermilk (page 34) Dressing
- 6 cups **MIXED GREENS**
- 1½ cups **CHERRY TOMATOES**, halved
- ½ **RED ONION**, thinly sliced
- 2 **AVOCADOS**, pits removed, quartered, and sliced
- 4 slices **BACON**, cooked and roughly chopped

Let's Toss!

1. Season the steak with salt and pepper on both sides.

2. Heat canola oil in a grill pan or a cast-iron skillet over medium-high heat.

3. Add steak and cook about 3 minutes each side.

4. Let steak rest on a plate under tented aluminum foil for about 5 minutes. Slice. (See tips for slicing steak, p. 146.)

STOP! SOAK GRILL PAN.

5. In a large glass bowl, mix 4 tablespoons of the dressing with the greens, tomatoes, and onions.

6. Set salad out on 4 large plates, evenly sprinkle with avocado and bacon, and top with steak slices.

TEX-MEX SALAD

Serves 4

PREP 6 minutes
COOK 7 minutes
CLEAN 5 minutes

I live in California, a state in which there is a huge Mexican influence, especially in cuisine. That means dishes that always balance a little citrus and produce with a powerful, spicy kick. This salad does just that, with a bonus of black beans to smooth things out a bit.

1 (15-ounce) can black beans
1 **JALAPEÑO**, seeded and finely diced
8 cups roughly chopped **ROMAINE LETTUCE**
2 cups shredded **CABBAGE**
1½ cups **CHERRY TOMATOES**, halved
1 teaspoon kosher salt
½ teaspoon freshly ground black pepper
½ cup Lime Avocado Dressing (page 28) or Stu's Super Citrus Vinaigrette (page 30)
1 two-pound **ROTISSERIE CHICKEN**, meat removed (about 3 cups)

Let's Toss!

1. Drain and rinse the black beans.

2. In a large glass bowl, combine black beans, jalapeño, romaine, cabbage, and cherry tomatoes along with the salt and pepper. Toss.

3. Add ½ cup of dressing and, using your hands, mix everything until the ingredients are lightly covered.

4. Divide evenly among 4 large plates. Top with rotisserie chicken. Serve.

Tip: Save time by purchasing cabbage that has already been shredded.

☆ Tip: Here's a time-saver. Preheating the baking pan speeds up the cooking time of vegetables.

KALE, FINGERLING POTATO, AND BACON SALAD

Serves 4
PREP 6 minutes
COOK 45 minutes
CLEAN 6 minutes

I've told you why I love kale; add some meat (bacon) and fingerling potatoes and you've got a balanced meal right in a salad. Walnuts bring extra texture and blue cheese gives a little funk to this great mix.

- 4 medium eggs
- 4 slices thick-cut **BACON**, roughly sliced
- ½ pound **BABY POTATOES**, sliced
- ½ teaspoon freshly ground black pepper
- ½ teaspoon kosher salt
- ½ pound **KALE** greens, stems removed
- 5 tablespoons Lime Avocado (page 28) or Balsamic (page 31) Dressing
- ¾ cup chopped **WALNUTS**
- ¾ cup **BLUE CHEESE** crumbles

Let's Toss!

1. Place a 26 x 18-inch rimmed baking sheet in the oven and preheat the oven to 400°F.

2. In a small saucepan, bring water to a boil. Once water is boiling, add eggs carefully and continue to boil for 6 minutes. Immediately remove from heat and rinse under cold water to cool. Peel and quarter eggs. Set aside.

3. In a large nonstick skillet over medium heat, cook bacon until crispy, about 8 minutes. Transfer bacon to a plate lined with a paper towel. Pour bacon fat into a heatproof glass bowl.

4. Add potatoes and pepper to the bacon fat. Remove the pan from the oven and drop the potato mixture onto the piping hot baking sheet. Roast for 30 minutes. The potatoes will begin to sear.

 **STOP!** CLEAN SUACEPAN AND SKILLET.

5. Take out potatoes and let cool. Season with salt.

6. Toss kale with 5 tablespoons of dressing and add the potatoes and bacon. Divide on plates and top with walnuts, egg, and cheese. Serve.

☆ Tip: Be sure not to salt potatoes until AFTER roasting so as not to draw moisture out of them too soon.

SIMPLE BREAD SALAD

Serves 4

PREP 5 minutes
COOK 15 minutes
CLEAN 4 minutes

I'm a big guy and I like to eat, so tossing some bread into a salad is a great idea. It adds some heartiness and I just love that the bread acts as a sponge of sorts for a great dressing.

½ of a 28-inch **BAGUETTE**, cut into 1-inch pieces

3 tablespoons extra virgin olive oil

¾ pound prewashed **MIXED LETTUCES**, such as baby arugula, red leaf, butter lettuce, and romaine

½ small **RED ONION**, thinly sliced

4 tablespoons Buttermilk (page 34) or Lime Avocado (page 28) Dressing

1 cup **CHERRY TOMATOES**, halved

1 (15-ounce) can **LENTILS**, drained

Let's Toss!

1. Place a 26 x 18-inch rimmed baking sheet in the oven and preheat the oven to 400°F.

2. In a bowl, toss baguette pieces with olive oil.

3. Carefully remove baking sheet from oven and spread bread out on the sheet. Place back into oven and toast bread for 8 to 10 minutes, or until golden brown. Set aside to cool.

4. Toss all the lettuces and the red onion with dressing. Divide among 4 plates. Top with croutons, tomatoes, and lentils.

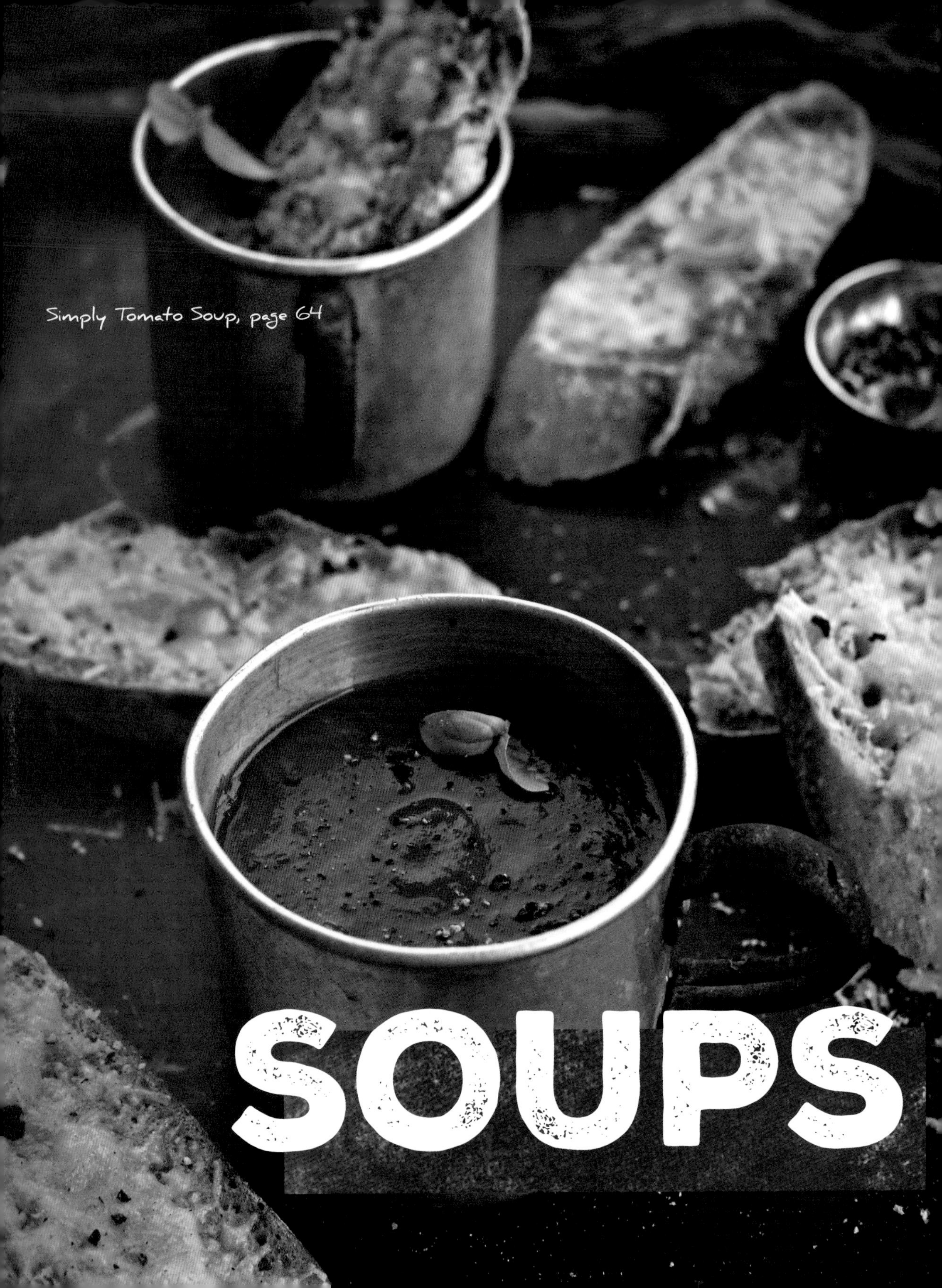

Simply Tomato Soup, page 64

When I think about soup, I think about growing up in Ireland and coming in from school on a cold winter's day. My mother would always have a big pot of chicken soup on the stove for the family whenever we wanted a bowl. Always sublime, it made me feel literally warm inside. And to me, soup can be a whole meal in its own right. Think about it—soup is just a big pot of flavors simmering together. These recipes are designed so that they can be done fast—no need to be checking on a stockpot for hours. They still have the great flavors I crave, yet made in a quarter of the time.

QUICK 6 TIPS FOR SOUPS

- Buy an immersion blender or, better still, a food processor to cut time and create beautiful, velvety soups.
- Soups freeze extremely well, so it's a good idea to double up on a batch, let the final product cool to room temperature, and freeze portions in airtight containers.
- Soups are a great way to use any leftover vegetables and lettuces. Chop up any leftover spinach, arugula, kale, or veggies and toss them in before they go bad. Sometimes it's nice to add some texture to your soups.
- If you have a few lemons around, squeeze a splash here and there into your soups. I always find that lemon juice gives soups a refreshing twist.
- Most important: always let soups cool for a bit—at least 10 minutes—before putting in a blender. Hot soups will rise up and explode from the blender!
- As it is for salads, a cooked rotisserie chicken is your secret weapon for some of these recipes, too! A precooked chicken adds a meaty element to your soups while saving you the trouble of cooking it! One 2-pound chicken will give you 3 cups of meat off the bone—2 cups of white meat and 1 cup of dark meat. Keep leftover chicken in a sealed container or Ziploc bag in the fridge for up to 4 days.

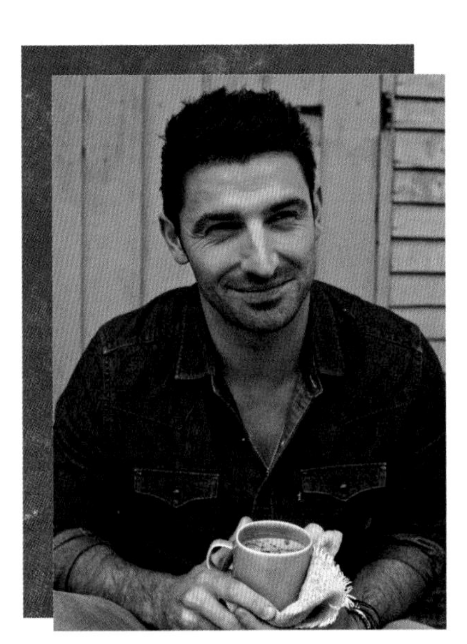

Tools

Blender (standard, immersion, or food processor)
Chef's knife
Cutting board
Dutch oven (large, 5-quart) or casserole dish (5-quart)
Ladle
Slotted spoon
Spatula
Stirring spoon
Whisk

3x
Remember the power of reading through a recipe 3 TIMES!

BACON, KALE, AND POTATO SOUP

Serves 6
PREP 6 minutes
COOK 30 minutes
CLEAN 6 minutes

Yes, I'm Irish, and yes, I live the potato-eating stereotype. Potatoes, like Guinness, are just in our blood. I just love potatoes, and forgive me for tooting my own horn, but I am pretty darn good at making anything that has them in it. In this recipe, the salty bacon, the cabbagy flavor of the kale, and the hearty potatoes hit me right in my Irish heart.

6 slices **BACON**, diced
1 medium onion, diced
1 pound **BABY POTATOES**, washed, skin on and halved
6 cups beef stock
1 tablespoon fresh **THYME** leaves
8 ounces (2 cups) **KALE**, roughly chopped
1 teaspoon kosher salt
1 teaspoon freshly ground black pepper

Let's Cook!

1. In a large nonstick stockpot or saucepan, sauté bacon over medium heat until crispy, about 5 to 7 minutes. Remove bacon from pan and set aside on a plate lined with paper towels.
2. Add onion to the pot or pan and cook for 3 minutes. Add potatoes, stock, and thyme.
3. Bring to a boil and let simmer for 15 minutes until the potatoes are tender.
4. Add the kale and simmer for 3 minutes more. Season with the salt and pepper.
5. Let soup cool for about 10 minutes before you ladle into a blender or food processor. Puree until smooth.
6. Reheat and ladle into bowls and top with bacon pieces.

WHITE BEAN CHICKEN SOUP

Serves 6–8

PREP 6 minutes

COOK 30 minutes

CLEAN 6 minutes

What I love most about this soup is its simplicity. The simple flavors of chicken and beans are easy comfort. And this soup is light on labor, so much so that I'll be frank: It's less about cooking and more about heating up good ingredients. Convenience is always key when you are pressed for time. This one is great as a quick lunch or snack when you are in a pinch.

- 1 medium yellow onion, diced
- 4 (15-ounce) cans cannellini beans, drained
- 6 cloves garlic, peeled and crushed
- 6 cups chicken stock
- 2 teaspoons kosher salt
- 1 teaspoon freshly ground black pepper
- 1 two-pound **ROTISSERIE CHICKEN**, meat removed (about 3 cups)
- 10 **BASIL** leaves, chopped
- 2 tablespoons fresh **PARSLEY**, chopped
- Extra virgin olive oil for garnish
- 4–6 **BASIL** leaves for garnish

Let's Cook!

1. In a large stockpot or saucepan over medium-high heat, add onion, beans, garlic, chicken stock, salt, and pepper; stir and bring to a simmer. This will take about 15 minutes.

2. Turn off heat and let soup cool for about 10 minutes. Scoop out 2 tablespoons of beans with a slotted spoon and set aside. Ladle remaining soup into a blender or food processor and puree.

3. Pour back into the large stockpot or saucepan and heat over medium heat.

4. Stir in the reserved beans, rotisserie chicken, basil, and parsley and heat for 5 more minutes.

5. Ladle into bowls and garnish with some extra virgin olive oil and basil leaves.

Tip: No need to peel the woody bottoms of asparagus. Simply snap off the bottoms, reserve, and cook the rest.

CHICKEN AND RICE MISO SOUP

Serves 6
PREP 6 minutes
COOK 30 minutes
CLEAN 4 minutes

I was first introduced to miso soup when I moved to California, and my world completely changed. Whenever I go out for sushi, I always start the meal with a steaming hot bowl of salty miso soup, no matter how hot it is outside in Los Angeles. It is also my go-to when I am feeling under the weather. Today I feel like miso has become so much a part of me that it would be utter madness if I didn't include it in my cookbook.

- ½ cup white or yellow **MISO PASTE**
- 1 tablespoon **FISH SAUCE**
- ½ tablespoon low-sodium soy sauce
- 8 cups water
- 1½ cups long-grain white rice, uncooked
- 1 two-pound **ROTISSERIE CHICKEN**, meat removed (about 3 cups)
- 10 **ASPARAGUS** spear tips, trimmed and cut into 1-inch pieces
- 1 teaspoon freshly ground black pepper
- 1 **GREEN ONION**, thinly sliced lengthwise

Let's Cook!

1. In a large stockpot or saucepan, heat miso paste, fish sauce, soy sauce, and water over medium-high heat. Cover and bring to a boil. Reduce heat and let simmer for 5 minutes.

2. Add rice and cook for 7 more minutes.

3. Add chicken and asparagus and cook for 2 more minutes.

4. Season with pepper, ladle into bowls, and sprinkle with green onions.

PEA AND HAM SOUP

Serves 6–8

PREP 6 minutes
COOK 30 minutes
CLEAN 6 minutes

My aunt Derry would make this soup while I was growing up. She's the person who made me love peas, simply steaming them and putting butter and salt over them. When Derry would bake a ham over the weekend, she would take chunks of the leftovers and throw them in a pea soup. She'd serve this lovely soup to me sometimes on a cold day after school. Every time I eat this I think back to being a kid, doing my homework at three-thirty in the afternoon, and enjoying a warming bowl.

6 thick slices **BACON**, cut into 1-inch chunks
1 medium onion, roughly chopped
4 cloves garlic, crushed
2 **CARROTS**, roughly diced
1 **CELERY** stalk, roughly diced
1 teaspoon kosher salt
1 teaspoon freshly ground black pepper
2 pounds **FROZEN PEAS**, thawed
7 cups chicken stock
Extra virgin olive oil for garnish

Let's Cook!

1. In a large nonstick stockpot or saucepan, cook bacon over medium-high heat until really crispy, about 5 to 7 minutes. Remove bacon and set aside.

2. Add onion, garlic, carrot, and celery to the pot and cook for 7 minutes, until everything softens.

3. Add the salt, pepper, peas, and chicken stock. Bring to a boil, reduce heat to medium, and simmer for 10 minutes.

4. Let soup cool for about 10 minutes, then ladle soup in batches into a blender or food processor and puree until smooth. Pour the soup back into the pot. Taste and season with more salt and pepper if needed.

5. Heat the soup, ladle into bowls, and sprinkle with bacon pieces. Drizzle with some extra virgin olive oil.

evening, and Hawkins
cards. Jeremiah
175

Tip: Want to keep this soup vegetarian? Sub in vegetable stock for the chicken stock.

BUTTERNUT SQUASH AND COCONUT SOUP

Serves 6

PREP 6 minutes

COOK 35 minutes

CLEAN 6 minutes

Thanksgiving time in the United States always reminds me how versatile butternut squash is. You can roast it, boil it, steam it, and puree it into soups just like this one. It also freezes well, so you can stock up over the autumn and stash them in the freezer to make this all-year-round. Or just find it in the frozen food section.

2 tablespoons canola oil

1 tablespoon unsalted butter

1 medium onion, diced

1 2-inch piece **GINGER**, peeled and chopped

4 cloves garlic, crushed

2 pounds frozen, cubed **BUTTERNUT SQUASH**, thawed

4 cups chicken stock or vegetable stock

1 teaspoon kosher salt

1 teaspoon freshly ground black pepper

1 (14-ounce) can coconut milk

1 tablespoon **THAI RED CURRY PASTE** (feel free to use more if you want to amp up the curry flavor)

1 handful **CILANTRO** for garnish

Let's Cook!

1. In a large stockpot or saucepan, heat oil and butter over medium-high heat. Add the onion and cook until softened, 5 minutes.

2. Add the ginger and garlic and cook for 2 minutes, stirring.

3. Add the squash, stock, salt, and pepper and bring to a boil over high heat. Reduce heat to medium and let simmer, covered, for 15 minutes.

4. Reserve 6 tablespoons of coconut milk for serving. Whisk the remainder of the coconut milk along with the red curry paste into the soup.

5. Turn off the heat and let the soup cool for about 10 minutes.

6. Ladle the soup into a food processor in batches and puree. Return the smooth soup to the pot, reheat, and serve warm in bowls. Sprinkle with cilantro leaves. Garnish with some extra coconut milk.

MY MOTHER'S CHICKEN NOODLE SOUP

Serves 6–8

PREP 6 minutes

COOK 30 minutes

CLEAN 6 minutes

My mother would make this classic for us at least once a week when the colder months came in Ireland. She would boil a whole chicken, add veggies, and make use of whatever pasta she had left in the pantry. This is my speedier version of her soup, which makes use of an already cooked chicken.

1 tablespoon canola oil

2 tablespoons unsalted butter

1 medium onion, diced

2 medium **CARROTS**, peeled and chopped

2 **CELERY** stalks, chopped

1 teaspoon dried chili flakes

1 teaspoon salt

1 teaspoon freshly ground black pepper

8 cups good quality chicken stock, such as Kitchen Basics

1 two-pound **ROTISSERIE CHICKEN**, meat removed (about 3 cups)

¾ pound bucatini pasta (or whichever pasta you like)

2 tablespoons chopped fresh **PARSLEY**

For serving: **CRUSTY BREAD**

Let's Cook!

1. In a large stockpot or saucepan, heat oil with butter over medium heat. Add onion, carrots, celery, and chili flakes and cook until softened, about 5 minutes.

2. Season with salt and pepper. Add chicken stock, turn heat up to high, and bring to a simmer for 10 minutes.

3. Add pasta. Turn up heat to medium-high and cook for 8 to 10 minutes or until pasta is al dente.

4. Add chicken to the pot. Reduce heat to medium. Continue cooking 2 minutes.

5. Ladle into big bowls, season to taste, and sprinkle with parsley. Serve with crusty bread.

Want to keep this soup vegetarian? Substitute vegetable stock for the chicken stock.

SWEET POTATO, LEMONGRASS, AND CILANTRO SOUP

Serves 6
PREP 6 minutes
COOK 30 minutes
CLEAN 6 minutes

As I mentioned, I love all things potato, including sweet potatoes, so of course I have a sweet potato soup recipe up my sleeve as well. This one brilliantly blends the flavors of East and West—with chicken stock bridging the sweetness of the yam with the aromatics of the lemongrass and cilantro.

- 4 tablespoons unsalted butter, plus more for serving
- 1 onion, peeled and chopped
- 6 large **SWEET POTATOES**, peeled and roughly chopped
- 1 tablespoon ground cumin
- 6 cups chicken stock or vegetable stock
- 4 **LEMONGRASS STALKS**
- 1 teaspoon kosher salt
- 1 teaspoon freshly ground black pepper
- 1 tablespoon **CILANTRO** leaves, for garnish
- For serving: **CRUSTY BREAD** and butter

Let's Cook!

1. In a large stockpot or saucepan, heat butter over medium heat. Add onions and soften for about 5 minutes, stirring.

2. Add the sweet potatoes and cumin together, stirring so everything is coated in butter and cumin.

3. Add chicken or vegetable stock, cover, and increase heat to medium-high.

4. Remove outer layer of lemongrass stalks and finely chop. Add to the pot and let simmer for 20 minutes.

5. Remove from heat and let soup cool for 10 minutes. Puree in a food processor until smooth. Add salt and pepper.

6. Return to pot, heat, and serve with warmed crusty bread and butter. Sprinkle soup with cilantro leaves.

Tip: Save prep time by purchasing frozen cubed sweet potatoes.

SIMPLY TOMATO SOUP

Serves 4–6

PREP 6 minutes
COOK 25 minutes
CLEAN 6 minutes

A classic! I love the tangy, sometimes sour flavors that come to the fore in this soup. A touch of butter gives this soup an extra bit of richness. I know for those raised in the United States, a cherished childhood memory often involves a lunch of a good tomato soup, usually paired with a grilled cheese sandwich. I think that's a perfect match.

¼ cup extra virgin olive oil
2 medium onions, diced
4 cloves garlic, chopped
1 teaspoon dried chili flakes
2 teaspoons kosher salt
2 teaspoons freshly ground black pepper
2 (28-ounce) cans diced San Marzano tomatoes
2 cups vegetable stock
1 tablespoon sugar
¾ cup shaved Parmesan
½ of a 28-inch **BAGUETTE**, sliced diagonally into 1-inch slices
2 tablespoons unsalted butter
10 **BASIL** leaves, torn

Let's Cook!

1. In a large pot or saucepan, heat oil over medium heat. Add onion, garlic, chili flakes, salt, and pepper. Stir and cook for about 5 to 7 minutes until onions have softened.

2. Add tomatoes, vegetable stock, and sugar together and simmer on medium-low heat for 10 minutes. Remove from heat.

3. Meanwhile, sprinkle Parmesan on bread and toast under the broiler until the cheese has melted, about 1 to 2 minutes. Set aside. (Don't walk away from it while it's cooking because it may burn.)

4. Puree the soup along with the butter until smooth. You can use an immersion blender, blender, or food processor to do this.

5. Return soup to the large pot or saucepan, stir in basil, and serve warm in bowls with some Parmesan toast.

PASTA

Tagliatelle with Mushy Peas, Pork Sausages, and Ricotta, page 79

I never order pasta in restaurants because I feel as if it's often overpriced for how cheap and easy it is to make at home. Personally, I'd rather add another ten dollars to my meal to get a steak or have a glass of wine.

QUICK SIX TIPS FOR PASTA

- Always try and buy a nice fresh handmade pasta, if possible. It freezes nicely before use and there's a tremendous difference in texture and flavor.
- Always cook pasta a minute less than directed on the package. It prevents overcooking when you are finishing pasta in a pan, and it's the best way to achieve a nice al dente texture.
- When you drain pasta, keep a little of the cooking water. You can use it to thicken the sauce, and the starch in the liquid also helps the sauce cling to the pasta.
- I like to toss pasta with a tablespoon of olive oil so it doesn't become sticky or clumpy.
- If you have leftover pasta, toss a little oil in before you put it in the fridge. This helps preserve it to serve another day and ensures that it will heat up again nicely.
- Get the water boiling before you start any pasta dish. This saves so much time while you organize yourself to get ready to start cooking.

Tools

Baking dish (3-quart)
Chef's knife
Cheese grater
Colander
Cutting board
Dutch oven or stockpot (large, 5- or 6-quart)
Pasta pot (large, 6-quart)
Skillets (8-inch, 10-inch, 12-inch, nonstick, 12-inch deep)
Spoon (wooden)
Saucepan (large, 4-quart)
Tongs
Whisk
Zester

3x
Remember the rule of three: Read recipes through 3 TIMES before you begin cooking!

PENNE with TOMATOES AND BACON

Serves 4
PREP 6 minutes
COOK 30 minutes
CLEAN 6 minutes

I like to think of this dish as a BLT in pasta form. The bacon adds a nice, salty, smoky edge to the sauce, which is balanced by the slight sweet of the sugar. This is just one of my feel-good recipes.

1 pound penne pasta
2 tablespoons olive oil
1 onion, finely chopped
4 slices **SMOKED BACON**, roughly chopped
½ teaspoon dried chili flakes
1 tablespoon tomato paste
½ cup white wine
1 teaspoon sugar
1 (28-ounce) can diced San Marzano tomatoes
½ teaspoon kosher salt
½ teaspoon freshly ground black pepper
4 tablespoons Parmesan cheese

Let's Cook!

1. Add 1 teaspoon of salt to a pot of water and bring to a boil. Cook the pasta for 1 minute less than the package instructs.
2. While the pasta is cooking, heat olive oil over medium-high heat in a large nonstick skillet until shimmering. Add onion, bacon, and chili flakes and cook until fat begins to render, about 8 minutes.
3. Add tomato paste, white wine, and sugar and bring to a simmer for 3 to 5 minutes over medium heat.
4. Add tomatoes and simmer for 10 more minutes. Season with salt and pepper.
5. When sauce has thickened, add drained pasta and toss with the sauce.
6. Divide onto 4 plates and sprinkle with Parmesan cheese.

FYI: Rendering the bacon means cooking the bacon until the white, fatty parts melt into grease.

ANGEL HAIR, SHRIMP, TOMATOES, AND LEMON

Serves 4

PREP 6 minutes

COOK 25 minutes

CLEAN 6 minutes

This dish is great because the ingredients are easy to obtain and available year-round. Then there's the flavor: The lemon zest adds a wonderful citrusy zing to the sweetness of the tomatoes, which is amped up with a bit of sugar. The shrimp adds a wonderful texture.

- 2 tablespoons extra virgin olive oil
- 3 cloves garlic, minced
- 2 tablespoons chopped fresh **BASIL**, plus extra leaves for garnish
- 2 teaspoons dried oregano
- Juice of 1 lemon
- 1 teaspoon lemon zest
- 1 tablespoon sugar
- ½ cup dry white wine
- 1 (28-ounce) can chopped San Marzano tomatoes
- ¾ pound angel hair or capellini pasta
- 20 uncooked large **SHRIMP**, peeled and deveined
- ½ teaspoon kosher salt
- ½ teaspoon freshly ground black pepper

Let's Cook!

1. Heat oil in a large skillet over medium heat. Add garlic, cook for 1 minute, then add chopped basil, oregano, lemon juice, zest, and sugar. Cook for about 1 minute longer until aromas develop.

2. Turn up the heat to medium-high, add wine, and let simmer for 1 minute. Add the tomatoes, stir, and let simmer for 15 minutes until sauce thickens.

3. Meanwhile, boil water in a large pot and cook pasta for 1 minute less than the package instructs. Strain in a colander and set aside.

4. Add shrimp to sauce and cook in the sauce for the last 3 minutes of cooking time.

5. Divide pasta among 4 bowls and top with sauce and shrimp. Season with salt and pepper. Garnish with extra basil leaves and serve.

Tip: Save time by always buying your shrimp peeled and deveined.

How to buy the best shrimp:

1. Smell it. The aroma should not be fishy. If it's fishy, it's old.

2. Check the texture. It should be firm, not limp.

3. To guarantee ultimate freshness, ask your fishmonger when the shrimp came in.

FAST BACON AND SHRIMP TAGLIATELLE

Serves 4
PREP 6 minutes
COOK 25 minutes
CLEAN 6 minutes

This is my surf-and-turf pasta. The addition of the spinach brings a fresh green element to this dish, which of course also includes my favorite combo—bacon and tomato.

1 pound tagliatelle pasta
6 slices **BACON**, roughly chopped
6 cloves garlic, minced
1 pound medium **SHRIMP**, peeled and deveined
4 cups baby **SPINACH**
1 cup **CHERRY TOMATOES**, halved
1 teaspoon kosher salt

Let's Cook!

1. Cook pasta 1 minute less than the package instructs. Drain, reserving about ¾ cup of the cooking liquid.

2. Meanwhile, in a large nonstick skillet over medium-high heat, cook bacon until crispy, about 8 to 10 minutes. Set bacon aside and keep drippings in pan.

3. Add garlic to drippings and cook for 20 to 30 seconds. Add shrimp and cook for about 1½ minutes on each side until done. Remove shrimp from pan and set aside.

4. Add the reserved pasta liquid to the pan and scrape any bits from the bottom of the pan. Boil for about 30 to 45 seconds.

5. Add pasta to the pan and cook for 1 minute. Add the spinach, tomatoes, shrimp, and salt (and cook for a further 1 to 2 minutes).

6. Crumble bacon on top and serve immediately in a large bowl for family-style sharing.

PENNE ARRABIATA

Serves 4–6

PREP 6 minutes

COOK 25 minutes

CLEAN 6 minutes

When it comes to anything spicy, I'm in. No questions asked. A good arrabiata sauce is vital when it comes to making this dish. You don't just add hot sauce—you must simmer the pepper flakes in the sauce to really release those alluring aromas and potent spiciness.

- 3 cloves garlic, minced
- 3 tablespoons olive oil
- 2 (28-ounce) cans chopped San Marzano tomatoes, drained
- 2 teaspoons dried chili flakes
- 1 teaspoon oregano
- ½ teaspoon kosher salt
- Juice of 1 lemon
- 1 pound penne pasta
- ¾ cup freshly grated Parmesan cheese
- 8 **BASIL** leaves, thinly sliced

Let's Cook!

1. In a large saucepan over medium-high heat, cook the garlic in olive oil for 1 to 2 minutes. Add tomatoes, bring to a simmer, then reduce heat to low.

2. Add the chili flakes, oregano, salt, and lemon juice. Let simmer for 15 to 20 minutes.

3. Meanwhile, bring a large pot of salted water to a boil and cook pasta 1 to 2 minutes less than the package instructs for al dente. Drain, reserving about ½ cup of pasta liquid.

4. Add pasta and water to the sauce and stir to cover the pasta in the spicy sauce.

5. Stir in Parmesan cheese and basil. Serve in large bowls. Garnish with extra basil leaves and Parmesan.

Tip: When buying dried herbs, try using them within six months. If you find your herbs are on the wane, toast them up in a dry pan for a few seconds before using. When using fresh herbs, stick them in a glass of water, stem side down, to keep fresh until use.

LEMONY ARTICHOKE SPAGHETTI

Serves 4

PREP 6 minutes
COOK 25 minutes
CLEAN 6 minutes

This dish comes together as quickly as it takes to boil the water for the pasta. It was inspired by a trip to Seattle's Pike Place Market. I came upon a fantastic marinated artichoke bar there, and the thought just struck me how tasty marinated artichokes might be in a pasta.

- 1 pound spaghetti
- 3 tablespoons extra virgin olive oil
- 2 cloves garlic, minced
- 1 medium **SHALLOT**, minced
- 1 (12-ounce) jar or can **ARTICHOKE HEARTS**, halved
- Zest of 1 lemon
- Juice of 1 lemon
- 1½ cups dry white wine, such as a chardonnay
- 2 tablespoons chopped **PARSLEY**, divided
- 6 **BASIL** leaves, chopped, divided
- 4 tablespoons unsalted butter
- ½ teaspoon salt
- ½ teaspoon freshly ground black pepper
- Freshly grated Parmesan cheese for garnish

Let's Cook!

1. Add 1 teaspoon of salt to a pot of water and bring to a boil. Cook the pasta for 1 minute less than the package instructs.

2. While the water is boiling, add the extra virgin olive oil to a large skillet and heat over medium-high heat. Add the garlic and shallot and sauté together for about 3 minutes.

3. Add the artichoke hearts, lemon zest, lemon juice, and white wine. Bring to a simmer for about 10 minutes, or until the liquid has reduced to half and coats the back of the spoon.

4. Stir in half the parsley and basil. Add the butter and let it melt into the sauce. Stir. Season with salt and pepper and turn down the heat on the sauce until pasta is ready.

5. When the pasta is cooked, drain and toss it in the skillet with the sauce and remaining parsley and basil.

6. Finish with some freshly grated Parmesan cheese and serve.

☆ Tip: Artichokes marinated in oil bring more flavor to this dish.

ANGEL HAIR with LEMON, KALE, AND PECANS

Serves 4–6
PREP 6 minutes
COOK 20 minutes
CLEAN 5 minutes

When kale started to take over the food world, I noticed it was juiced, made into chips, put into smoothies, and even sneaked into chocolate bars. So why not put it in a pasta dish? The nuts in this recipe give the dish another layer of flavor and a nice crunchy texture. The bitter, citrus, crunch, and chili all combine for a unique pasta.

- ½ cup **PECANS**
- 1 pound angel hair pasta
- ½ cup extra virgin olive oil, divided
- 4 cloves garlic, minced
- ½ teaspoon dried chili flakes
- ½ pound **KALE**, stems discarded and chopped
- Zest of 1 lemon
- Juice of 1 lemon
- 8 **BASIL** leaves, torn
- 2 teaspoons kosher salt
- 2 teaspoons freshly ground black pepper
- 4 tablespoons grated Parmesan

Let's Cook!

1. Toast pecans in a dry nonstick skillet over medium heat for 3 minutes until fragrant. Remove from skillet and chop. Set aside.

2. Add 1 teaspoon of salt to a pot of water and bring to a boil. Cook the pasta for 1 minute less than the package instructs.

3. While the pasta is cooking, heat ¼ cup olive oil over medium-high heat in a large nonstick skillet until shimmering. Add the garlic and chili flakes and stir for 30 seconds until fragrant.

4. Add kale and lemon zest and cook for 2 minutes more. Stir carefully so that the kale will not fall out of the pan.

5. Add the pasta, remaining olive oil, lemon juice, basil, salt, and pepper. Toss until everything is coated.

6. Portion pasta onto plates. Sprinkle with the pecans and Parmesan cheese.

FYI: Keep in mind that angel hair pasta is very thin and cooks very quickly.

FYI: Toasting nuts releases their natural oils and flavors.

TAGLIATELLE with MUSHY PEAS, PORK SAUSAGES, AND RICOTTA

Serves 4
PREP 6 minutes
COOK 20 minutes
CLEAN 6 minutes

For me, the best part of a good old-fashioned Irish breakfast is the sausage. And what better way to Irish up a pasta than with mushy peas? Add in ricotta and the noodles become extra creamy.

- 1 pound tagliatelle or your favorite pasta
- 3 tablespoons olive oil
- 4 cloves garlic, chopped
- ½ pound **BREAKFAST SAUSAGES**, casings removed
- 10 ounces **FROZEN PEAS**, thawed
- 6 ounces **RICOTTA**
- ½ teaspoon dried chili flakes
- 10 fresh **BASIL** leaves, chopped, plus extra for garnish
- ½ cup freshly grated Parmesan cheese
- ½ teaspoon salt
- ½ teaspoon freshly ground black pepper

Let's Cook!

1. Cook pasta 1 minute less than the package instructs. Drain, reserving about ¾ cup of the cooking liquid.

2. Meanwhile, in a large saucepan, heat olive oil over medium-high heat and add the garlic and sausage. Cook for about 3 to 5 minutes, breaking up sausage in the pan with a wooden spoon until browned all over. Remove and set aside.

3. Add the peas to the pan, and using a fork, lightly mash the peas. Turn heat to low.

4. Add ricotta, chili flakes, and 2 tablespoons of the cooking liquid to thicken the sauce. Add the cooked pasta and toss to coat, adding more cooking liquid if needed.

5. Return the sausage to the pan. Add the basil, Parmesan, salt, and pepper. Toss gently to coat and serve immediately, sprinkled with extra basil leaves.

MEDITERRANEAN TOMATO PASTA

Serves 4
PREP 6 minutes
COOK 20 minutes
CLEAN 6 minutes

The sun-dried tomatoes and Greek yogurt in this dish makes this very Mediterranean, adding a lovely tartness—something I discovered a bit by accident. I originally wanted to use some crème fraîche or sour cream, and when I couldn't find any, I tossed in Greek yogurt instead. I loved the result.

- 1 pound spaghetti or your favorite pasta
- 4 tablespoons olive oil
- 6 cloves garlic, minced
- 1 cup **SUN-DRIED TOMATOES**, finely chopped
- 1½ cups **CHERRY TOMATOES**, halved
- 1 cup nonfat plain **GREEK YOGURT**
- ½ teaspoon salt
- ½ teaspoon freshly ground black pepper
- 2 cups **ARUGULA**
- ½ teaspoon dried chili flakes

Let's Cook!

1. Cook pasta 1 minute less than the package instructs. Drain, reserving about ¾ cup of the cooking liquid.

2. While the pasta is cooking, heat olive oil over medium-high heat in a large skillet. Add garlic and sun-dried tomatoes. Cook for about 2 minutes. Lower the heat of the pan to medium-low.

3. Whisk in the plain Greek yogurt a tablespoon at a time. Whisk fast so it does not curdle. Warm through over medium heat.

4. Season with salt and pepper, then add in arugula, tomatoes, and the cooked pasta. Turn off heat and combine until pasta is well coated in the sauce. Add some of the reserved water to smoothen the sauce. Top with chili flakes and serve.

Tip: You can substitute crème fraîche or sour cream for the Greek yogurt in this pasta if you wish.

Tip: To make this dish vegetarian, use canola oil in place of bacon.

STUART'S IRISH YANKEE MAC AND CHEESE

Serves 6–8

PREP 6 minutes
COOK 40 minutes
CLEAN 6 minutes

I suppose this dish reflects my personality—after living in the United States for so many years, I've truly become an Irish Yank! This version of mac and cheese blends my two homes, with Irish dairy in a classic American dish.

- 1 pound elbow macaroni or your favorite pasta
- 1 tablespoon canola oil (if eliminating bacon for vegetarian version)
- 5 slices **BACON**, diced
- 4 cloves garlic, minced
- 4 tablespoons butter
- 4 tablespoons all-purpose flour
- 4½ cups milk
- 6 cups grated **SHARP WHITE CHEDDAR CHEESE**
- 1 teaspoon salt
- 1 teaspoon freshly ground black pepper
- 2 cups **FROZEN PEAS**, thawed
- 1 cup grated Parmesan cheese

Let's Cook!

1. Preheat the oven to 375°F.

2. Bring a pot of salted water to a boil and cook pasta 2 minutes less than the package instructs. Set aside.

3. In a large nonstick skillet, cook the bacon until it begins to crisp, about 4 to 5 minutes. Add garlic, cook for 1 more minute. Remove garlic and bacon and set aside.

4. In the same skillet, melt butter over medium heat. Whisk in the flour and cook for 1 minute until a paste forms. Continuously whisking, add the milk in slow increments until incorporated into the flour paste. Cook until thick and smooth, about 8 to 10 minutes.

5. Add in the cheddar cheese in thirds, until it has melted and becomes a velvety sauce. Season with salt and pepper. Add the macaroni, peas, and bacon-garlic mixture to the sauce.

6. Pour and scrape the macaroni into a 13 x 9-inch baking dish, sprinkle with Parmesan, and place in the preheated oven for about 20 minutes. Serve.

Package-Parceled Cod, page 94

As with a lot of kids, I didn't like fish when I was growing up. But when I began to travel and started to sample more fresh fish than what was available in my landlocked hometown, I realized what I was missing out on. Today fish is among my favorite things to eat. I love shopping for it, admiring the shiny fillets of halibut or the pinkish orange flesh of salmon at the market. I also love the fresh flavor of the sea. But the best part of fish, I discovered, is that it is so darned quick and easy to make. My simple, fast recipes are a great example of how refreshingly uncomplicated cooking fish can be.

STU'S GUIDE TO BUYING FISH PORTIONS

WHOLE OR ROUND FISH (SUCH AS COD OR BASS): ¾ to 1 pound per person

DRESSED OR CLEANED FISH (SUCH AS TROUT OR SNAPPER): ½ pound per person

FILLETS AND STEAKS (SUCH AS TUNA AND SALMON): ⅓ to ½ pound per person

MUSSELS: 12–15 per person

LOBSTER: 1–2 pounds per person

OYSTERS: 6 per person, depending on size

CLAMS: 8, depending on size

SHRIMP: 6–8, depending on size

SCALLOPS: 4–6, depending on size

How to tell if a fish is fresh? It should not smell fishy and the eyes should be clear and bright, not cloudy. The skin should be firm and the edges of the fish should not be dried or discolored.

STU'S GUIDE TO COOKING FISH

Time is the most important factor when it comes to cooking seafood. Overcooked fish becomes dry and inedible. Watch the clock carefully to ensure moist fish!

THE TEN-MINUTE RULE TO COOKING FISH

First, measure the fish for thickness. If stuffing fish, measure it after it is stuffed. Then plan on 10 minutes per inch of thickness *total*. So a piece of fish that is 1 inch thick requires 5 minutes cooking per side. (Sometimes I even like to knock a minute off each side for an extra-tender fish.)

Remember, forewarned is forearmed! Read recipes all the way through before starting.

3x

Three times is the charm.

Tools

- **Baking sheet** (rimmed, 18" x 13")
- **Bowls of various sizes**
- **Chef's knife**
- **Cutting board**
- **Dutch oven** (large, 5-quart, or casserole, 5-quart)
- **Food processor**
- **Ladle**
- **Parchment paper**
- **Skillet** (nonstick, 12-inch)
- **Spatula**
- **Spoon** (wooden)
- **Tongs**
- **Whisk**

QUICK SIX TIPS FOR FISH

- Remove fish from refrigerator 15 minutes before cooking to ensure even cooking.
- Thin fish (fish less than ½ inch thick) do not need to be turned over.
- When cooking frozen fish, double the cooking time but use a lower heat to avoid burning the outside and ending up with a raw center.
- Fish is done when it turns from translucent to opaque.
- Have your sides cooked and ready to go before you start to cook your fish. Fish should be eaten as soon as you are finished cooking it!
- When planning to serve fish, buy it the day you intend to cook it.

PAN-SEARED COD with SUCCOTASH

Serves 4

PREP 6 minutes

COOK 20 minutes

CLEAN 6 minutes

This recipe is so easy you can cook it in the dark with one hand. Literally. I know because I did exactly that when I made this recipe for a charity dinner. It was a "Dining in the Dark" event . . . and I had a broken arm from a motorcycle accident. Thankfully, I had a sous-chef to prep the onion, garlic, tomatoes, and basil. But I was able to do the rest with one arm.

- 3 tablespoons canola oil, divided
- 1 medium yellow onion, chopped
- 2 cloves garlic, minced
- 1 teaspoon dried chili flakes
- 2 cups **FROZEN CORN**, thawed
- 1 (10-ounce) package **FROZEN LIMA BEANS**, thawed
- 1 cup **CHERRY TOMATOES**, halved
- 2 tablespoons cider vinegar
- 10 **BASIL** leaves, roughly chopped, plus extra for garnish
- 4 6-ounce **COD FILLETS**, 1 inch thick, skinless
- 1 teaspoon kosher salt
- 1 teaspoon freshly ground black pepper

Let's Cook!

1. Heat 2 tablespoons canola oil over medium-high heat in a large nonstick skillet. Add onion, lower heat to medium, and cook for 5 minutes or until onion is softened.

2. Add garlic and chili flakes together to the pan and cook for 1 minute.

3. Stir in corn, lima beans, and tomatoes and cook until tomatoes start to soften, about 4 to 6 minutes. Stir in vinegar and basil. Cover and keep warm.

4. In another large nonstick skillet, heat remaining 1 tablespoon canola oil until beginning to shimmer.

5. Season cod on both sides with salt and pepper. Then place fish carefully into pan, rolling the fish away from you so the oil does not splatter. Cook on each side for 3 to 4 minutes until cooked all the way through.

6. Spoon succotash onto plates. Place fish on top. Garnish with some extra fresh basil leaves and serve.

SPEEDY CIOPPINO

Serves 4
PREP 6 minutes
COOK 35 minutes
CLEAN 6 minutes

When I began my journey in the United States, I lived in the small town of St. Helena in the Napa Valley. I worked in a hotel up there, and that is where I had my first cioppino, a fish stew that originated in San Francisco. Cioppino is very much like bouillabaisse, except with a spicy tomato-based broth instead of saffron. Both dishes have an abundance of various fresh fish, so feel free to add whatever you can find that's freshest in your market.

- 3 tablespoons olive oil
- 1 medium onion, diced
- 6 cloves garlic, crushed
- 1 teaspoon kosher salt
- 1 teaspoon freshly ground black pepper
- 2 teaspoons dried chili flakes
- 1½ cups dry white wine (I use chardonnay)
- 1 (28-ounce) can diced San Marzano tomatoes
- 2 pounds **SEAFOOD** (I like a combination of cod, halibut, mussels, and scallops. Cut the cod and halibut into 1-inch pieces)
- 1 crusty French **BAGUETTE**, torn into 4 pieces
- 10 medium **BASIL** leaves, chopped, as garnish

Let's Cook!

1. In a large Dutch oven or heavy pot, heat oil over medium heat. Add onion and garlic and cook for 3 minutes.

2. Add salt, pepper, and chili flakes and cook for 1 minute.

3. Add wine and let simmer for 2 minutes. Add the tomatoes and 1 cup water, cover, and let simmer over medium heat for about 10 to 15 minutes.

4. Remove the lid and add all the seafood, give a quick stir, place the lid back on, and cook for another 5 minutes, or until shells have opened.

5. Ladle into big bowls, sprinkle with basil, and serve with crusty bread and butter.

CHOWDERED SCALLOPS

Serves 4

PREP 6 minutes

COOK 30 minutes

CLEAN 6 minutes

Scallops are really easy to cook and they take wonderfully to chowder. Bacon adds a smoky base to the hearty dish, while corn brings a touch of sweetness.

4 slices **BACON**, chopped

16 medium **SEA SCALLOPS**, patted dry

1 teaspoon kosher salt

1 teaspoon freshly ground black pepper

2 **SHALLOTS**, minced

6 **YUKON GOLD POTATOES**, cut into ½-inch cubes

¾ cup chicken broth

½ cup heavy cream

1½ cups **FROZEN CORN**, thawed

2 tablespoons chopped **PARSLEY**

Let's Cook!

1. In a large nonstick skillet over medium-high heat, cook the bacon for about 4 to 5 minutes until crispy. Remove bacon and reserve 1 tablespoon of bacon fat in the pan.

2. Season scallops with salt and pepper.

3. Over medium heat, cook the scallops about 2 minutes each side until golden. Set aside on a plate covered with tented foil.

4. Add the shallots to the pan and cook for 3 minutes.

5. Add potatoes, broth, and cream together. Bring to a simmer and cook for 12 minutes or until potatoes are tender. Add the corn and scallops to the pan and cook for a further 3 minutes.

6. Place 4 scallops on each plate. Spoon sauce over and sprinkle with parsley and bacon.

☆ Tip: If you end up with leftover bacon fat, here's a delicious way to reuse it: Make Bacon Parm popcorn! Add 1/4 cup bacon fat to 1/4 cup popcorn kernels. Pop and grate some fresh Parmesan cheese on top.

TEN-MINUTE COCONUT SHRIMP CURRY

Serves 4
PREP 6 minutes
COOK 10 minutes
CLEAN 6 minutes

I'm a big fan of coconut and an even bigger fan of coconut curry. Coconut milk adds another layer of flavor and a smooth texture to any curry base. Red curry and coconut go together particularly well with seafood. Shrimp is the perfect ingredient to stand up to the complex, powerful spices of this red curry sauce. And yes, this does take only 10 minutes to make, I promise!

- 1 teaspoon canola oil
- 2 tablespoons **RED CURRY PASTE** (feel free to add more if you want to amp up the curry flavor)
- 1 (14-ounce) can coconut milk
- 1 teaspoon dried chili flakes
- 1 **RED BELL PEPPER**, deseeded and cut into strips
- 2 cups **BUTTON MUSHROOMS**, halved
- 24 uncooked **SHRIMP**, peeled and deveined
- 10 fresh **BASIL** leaves
- 1 teaspoon kosher salt
- 1 teaspoon freshly ground black pepper

Let's Cook!

1. In a large skillet, heat canola oil over medium-high heat. As soon as the oil begins to shimmer, whisk in the red curry paste and cook for about 1 minute. (This opens up the flavors of the paste.)
2. Pour in the coconut milk and continue whisking to combine the paste with the milk. Simmer for about 2 minutes.
3. Add chili flakes, red bell pepper, and mushrooms and cook, stirring for about 3 to 4 minutes.
4. Add the shrimp to the curry sauce and cook for another 3 minutes.
5. Stir in the basil, salt, and pepper. Serve over steamed rice.

PACKAGE-PARCELED COD

Serves 4

PREP 6 minutes
COOK 15 minutes
CLEAN 6 minutes

People often ask me the best way to ensure that you don't overcook a fish. The answer is to use my secret weapon: parchment paper. When you are cooking a fish in parchment, there's no worry about its sticking to the grill, cleanup is a breeze, and the parchment seals in moisture and flavor. Plus, there's a sort of Zen to folding the fish within the paper.

16 **ASPARAGUS SPEARS**, trimmed 1 inch from the ends
4 6-ounce **COD FILLETS**
1 lemon, sliced into 4 rounds
1 teaspoon kosher salt
1 teaspoon freshly ground black pepper
¼ cup lemon juice (about 3 lemons)
4 tablespoons extra virgin olive oil
4 sprigs fresh **THYME**

Let's Cook!

1. Preheat the oven to 350°F.

2. Lay out 1 large sheet (about 16" x 12") of parchment paper. Place 4 asparagus spears in the center of the paper, then 1 fish fillet on top, then a slice of lemon. Season with salt and pepper, 1 tablespoon of lemon juice, 1 tablespoon extra virgin olive oil, and 1 sprig of thyme.

3. Fold over the ends of the paper to enclose the fish.* Place on a baking sheet. Repeat with remaining fish.

4. Bake in the oven for about 12 to 15 minutes, or until fish reaches 130°F to 135°F on a thermometer.

SIDE DISH SUGGESTIONS: Soy Bok Choy (p. 182)

*How to Fold Parchment:
Place fish and vegetables in the center of the parchment sheet. Fold in two sides of the paper to the center, then smooth down and crease the sides until the paper stays. Do the same for the remaining two sides, smoothing down and creasing the paper until it stays in place.

Tip: Save time by asking your fishmonger to pick out the debearded mussels.

MOULES FRITES

Serves 4

PREP 6 minutes

COOK 20 minutes

CLEAN 6 minutes

When I lived in France for six months back in the summer of 2003, I worked fourteen-hour days—harder than I ever had in all my life. In the process, I discovered what a small piece of hell was like. At the end of it all, I took myself down to Biarritz in the Southwest of France to enjoy a week in the sun with my friend Eveanna. While there, I discovered a small piece of heaven in the moules frites. They were so plump and fresh, and the fries were perfectly crispy and salty. They were so good, we ate them practically every night. This recipe is my attempt to replicate that piece of heaven. It takes me right back to 2003.

4 tablespoons unsalted butter

2 large **SHALLOTS**, peeled and minced

6 cloves garlic, minced

2 teaspoons kosher salt

½ bottle of white wine (chardonnay is good)

¼ cup chopped **PARSLEY**

3 pounds **MUSSELS**, rinsed

Let's Cook!

1. In a large pot or Dutch oven, melt the butter over medium heat. Add the shallots, garlic, and salt and cook for 4 minutes, until shallots are softened.

2. Add the wine and parsley and bring to a boil.

3. Add the mussels and give them a good stir so they become coated with the liquid. Place the lid on the pot and let steam for about 5 minutes, until the shells open up. Lift the lid off and give them another stir. Cook for 3 minutes longer.

4. Serve in big bowls and ladle sauce into each. Serve with Crispy Fingerling Fries or a warmed, crusty baguette.

SIDE DISH SUGGESTIONS: Crispy Fingerling Fries (p. 166)

Tip: Start cooking this recipe when the fries are in their last 10 minutes of roasting.

CRISPY SALMON with PISTACHIO BASIL BUTTER

Serves 4

PREP 6 minutes

COOK 15 minutes

CLEAN 6 minutes

A compound butter is basically a fancy way of mashing butter with your favorite ingredient. The combinations of flavors in a compound butter are endless. This one matches perfectly with salmon, and the nutty crunch from the pistachio is a nice surprise.

¼ cup shelled **PISTACHIOS**

8 **BASIL** leaves

Juice of 1 lime

½ teaspoon dried chili flakes

2 teaspoons salt, plus ¼ teaspoon for fish

2 teaspoons freshly ground black pepper, plus ¼ teaspoon for fish

6 tablespoons unsalted butter, at room temperature

4 6-ounce **SALMON FILLETS**

1 tablespoon canola oil

Let's Cook!

1. Preheat the oven to 375°F.

2. In a food processor, pulse pistachios first, then add basil, lime juice, chili flakes, salt, pepper, and unsalted butter and pulse again for 5 seconds. Scoop out into a bowl. (This can be made up to 3 days in advance, covered, and refrigerated.)

3. Using a paper towel, pat dry and season salmon with ¼ teaspoon each of salt and pepper.

4. Heat canola oil in a large ovenproof skillet over medium-high heat.

5. Cook fish for 3 minutes per side. Place in the oven and finish cooking for 4 to 5 minutes

STOP! CLEAN FOOD PROCESSOR.

6. Remove the pan from oven and add the basil pistachio butter to the pan. Let butter melt and turn fish in butter to coat. Garnish with extra basil leaves, chopped pistachios, and some lime wedges.

SIDE DISH SUGGESTIONS: Minty Peas (p. 169), Parceled Lemony Asparagus (p. 171), Slow Roasted Cherry Tomatoes (p. 178)

JUMBO SHRIMP ROLL with SPICY CHILE BUTTER

Serves 4
PREP 4 minutes
COOK 15 minutes
CLEAN 6 minutes

I love a good lobster roll. But let's face it, lobster can be expensive, especially if you want to cook for a few friends or family. And while friends and family are important, you do have to pay your bills, too! This recipe replicates all of the lusciousness of lobster along with the extra zing of chile, while saving a few pennies, too.

3 tablespoons canola oil
20 medium **SHRIMP**, peeled and deveined
5 cloves garlic, chopped
1 teaspoon dried chili flakes
4 tablespoons unsalted butter
Juice of 2 lemons
2 tablespoons chopped **CILANTRO**
1 teaspoon kosher salt
1 teaspoon freshly ground black pepper
4 brioche **HAMBURGER BUNS**, sliced in half
2 cups **ARUGULA**

Let's Cook!

1. In a large skillet, heat canola oil over medium-high heat. Add shrimp and cook for about 2 to 3 minutes on each side (you may need to cook in two batches). Remove from the pan and set aside, covered.

2. In the same pan, add garlic and chili flakes and cook for 30 seconds.

3. Add butter, lemon juice, and cilantro. Stir, then add back in shrimp, turn off heat, and toss until covered. Season with salt and pepper.

4. Open brioche rolls and toast under the broiler, about 1 minute, until lightly golden.

5. Remove rolls from oven. Layer with arugula first, then 5 shrimp on each roll. Spoon over extra melted butter from the pan. Repeat with all buns. Serve.

SIDE DISH SUGGESTIONS: Crispy Fingerling Fries (p. 166), BBQ Baked Beans (p. 194), Mexican Street Corn (p. 188)

Thirteen-Spice Chicken with Crème Fraîche, page 117

When you are cooking for a group of friends or family, chicken is probably the easiest and cheapest way to go. Plus, I like the diversity that the different chicken parts offer, the intense flavor and succulence of the dark meat and the ease with which white meat can take on any flavor.

QUICK SIX TIPS FOR CHICKEN

- Citrus is a great go-to for chicken. It works wonderfully with orange, lemon, and lime zest. Thyme is a prime herb to pair with chicken, and garlic is also excellent for flavoring chicken.
- In order to ensure a juicy breast, sear on high heat, but always reduce the heat after the breast is brown or finish in the oven for a few minutes to cook the breast through.
- Don't shy away from bone-in cuts. Bones keep moisture in the meat!
- Test doneness by piercing the chicken with a skewer. When the juices run clear, not pink, you are good to go. **Important**: Chicken should register 165 degrees on a meat thermometer for a safe doneness.
- Always use a separate cutting board for poultry to avoid cross-contamination.
- When you are shopping for chicken, here are some words you should know. *Free-range* means that the chicken has been allowed access to the world outside of a cage. *Organic* means that 100 percent of the chicken's feed has been free from chemical fertilizers, fungicides, herbicides, and GMOs for at least three years. *Antibiotic-free* and *hormone-free* simply mean that the chickens are not given antibiotics and growth hormones.

Use your butcher! Save time and have your butcher cut your chicken into parts.

Tip: It's a good idea to invest in an oven thermometer so that you can gauge the true temperature of your oven. Note that cooking times can vary from oven to oven. Use your meat thermometer to determine doneness.

Tools

Aluminum foil

Baking sheet (rimmed, 18″ x 13″)

Chef's knife

Cutting board

Dutch oven (large, 5-quart, or casserole, 5-quart)

Meat thermometer

Skillets (nonstick, 12-inch, ovenproof, 12-inch)

Spatula

Spoon (wooden)

Tongs

Whisk

Ziploc bags

3x

Remember the power of reading through a recipe 3 TIMES!

CURRIED CHICKEN DINNER

Serves 4

PREP 6 minutes

COOK 40 minutes

CLEAN 6 minutes

Curry and chicken go together like bread and butter, while yogurt is the perfect avenue for infusing that wonderful, exotic flavor into the meat. Yogurt makes a great marinade in general, but especially for chicken. The enzymes in the yogurt break down the chicken and make it nice and moist. Marinating it right in a Ziploc bag also helps for an easy cleanup.

1 whole **CHICKEN**, cut into 10 pieces (get your butcher to do this)

2½ cups plain whole milk **GREEK YOGURT**

Juice of 2 lemons

3 tablespoons **CURRY POWDER**

1 tablespoon **CUMIN**

2 tablespoons **SESAME OIL** or canola oil

1 teaspoon dried chili flakes

1 teaspoon sea salt

1 teaspoon freshly ground black pepper

Let's Cook!

1. Preheat the oven to 400°F.

2. Pat chicken dry with paper towels. Place all chicken in one large Ziploc bag.

3. Add yogurt, lemon juice, curry powder, cumin, oil, chili flakes, salt, and pepper to the chicken in the bag. Close the bag. Toss with your hands so the marinade completely covers the chicken. Let marinate for 20 to 30 minutes.

4. Line a rimmed baking sheet with foil. Spread the chicken on the sheet, careful not to overcrowd.

5. Bake in the oven for about 20 to 25 minutes, or until meat registers 165 degrees on a meat thermometer. Serve over steamed rice.

CHICKEN RISOTTO

Serves 4
PREP 6 minutes
COOK 30 minutes
CLEAN 6 minutes

Risotto is so soothing; I think it's the epitome of creamy comfort. I love the depth that chicken adds to this dish, but you can also make it vegetarian by leaving out the meat.

- 9 cups chicken stock
- 2 tablespoons olive oil
- 3 medium boneless, skinless **CHICKEN BREASTS**, diced
- 2½ cups **ARBORIO RICE**
- 4 tablespoons unsalted butter
- 1 medium yellow onion, diced
- 1 cup chardonnay wine
- 12 **ASPARAGUS** spears, ends removed and cut into 1-inch pieces
- 1 teaspoon kosher salt
- 1 teaspoon freshly ground black pepper
- ½ cup grated Parmesan cheese for garnish

Let's Cook!

1. In a saucepan, bring chicken stock just to a boil over high heat. Once it boils, turn heat to low to keep it hot.

2. Add extra virgin olive oil to a Dutch oven or large pot over high heat. When oil starts to shimmer, add diced chicken and cook for about 5 minutes, until browned on all sides. Remove chicken and set aside.

3. Add rice to pot and let toast slightly for a minute. Add butter and cook until melted. Add onion and cook until translucent, about 3 to 5 minutes, stirring slowly with a wooden spoon. Reduce heat to a medium low. Add wine and let the rice absorb. Now add the chicken stock in cupful additions, waiting each time for the rice to absorb before adding another cup. Repeat until rice becomes creamy.

4. Taste. If the rice is too crunchy, start to add some hot water ½ cup at a time. Rice should ultimately be al dente, with just a slight bite to it. When this stage is achieved, add asparagus and chicken and stir for 3 to 5 minutes, until asparagus is fork tender but not limp.

5. Turn off heat. Add salt and pepper. Place about a cupful in the center of a plate and garnish with a tablespoon of grated fresh Parmesan cheese.

Tip: Attentiveness and stirring are the two keys to making a successful risotto! Do not walk away from the pot while making this. Stay over it and keep it on low heat, barely bubbling (never an agitated bubble), all the time. You want your resulting rice to have a small bite, and not end up with the texture of rice pudding.

BUFFALO CHICKEN WINGS, MAYTAG BLUE CHEESE DIPPING SAUCE

Serves 4

PREP 3 minutes
COOK 25 minutes
CLEAN 3 minutes

These wings are my guilty pleasure—there is something about buffalo chicken wings and a wickedly good hot sauce, particularly Frank's. During college I worked in a restaurant in Dublin. The wings they made there would rival those found in any American bar. I studied what they were doing very closely, and I think this recipe is the perfect facsimile.

2 pounds chicken **WING PIECES**

¾ cup **FRANK'S REDHOT HOT CAYENNE PEPPER SAUCE**

4 tablespoons unsalted butter, melted

¼ cup white wine vinegar

4 ounces **MAYTAG BLUE CHEESE** (or another good blue cheese)

1 cup **SOUR CREAM**

8 **CELERY** stalks, ends trimmed

Let's Cook!

1. Preheat oven to 450°F.

2. Line a 36 x 18-inch rimmed baking sheet with foil. Spread chicken wings out on baking sheet, making sure they do not overlap. (You want just one layer.) If needed, use a second baking sheet.

3. Roast in the oven for 20 to 25 minutes until crispy.

4. Meanwhile in a bowl, mix hot sauce, butter, and vinegar together. Set aside.

5. In a separate bowl, mix blue cheese and sour cream together. Set aside.

6. Toss the crispy wings in the bowl with the hot sauce. Serve with celery stalks and blue cheese dip.

SIDE DISH SUGGESTIONS: Crispy Fingerling Fries (p. 166), Buttermilk Dressing (p. 34)

THREE-BEAN BEER CHICKEN

Serves 4

PREP 6 minutes
COOK 25 minutes
CLEAN 6 minutes

One night I had a bunch of cut-up chicken pieces in my fridge, left over from a party the previous night. I had a bunch of beer left over, too. I put those two together, grabbed some beans I had on hand, and the result was this hearty stew.

- 1 2-to 3-pound **CHICKEN**, cut up into 10 pieces
- 3 tablespoons Old Bay seasoning
- 3 tablespoons unsalted butter
- 1 large onion, finely chopped
- 6 cloves garlic, minced
- 1 teaspoon kosher salt
- 1 teaspoon freshly ground black pepper
- 1 (28-ounce) can diced San Marzano tomatoes
- 1 (12-ounce) bottle of **LAGER BEER**
- 2 cups chicken stock
- 1 (15-ounce) can black beans, drained
- 1 (15-ounce) can cannellini beans, drained
- 1 (15-ounce) can **CHICKPEAS**, drained
- Garnish: 1 tablespoon chopped **PARSLEY**

Let's Cook!

1. Preheat oven to 375°F.

2. Pat chicken dry, then toss in a bowl with Old Bay seasoning. Roast on a rimmed baking sheet, lined with foil, in the oven for 15 minutes.

Tip: Have your butcher cut up the chicken for you or buy already cut chicken pieces.

3. Meanwhile, in a large Dutch oven or skillet, melt butter over medium heat. Sauté the onion and garlic together for about 3 to 4 minutes. Season with salt and pepper.

4. Remove chicken from oven and set aside.

5. Add the tomatoes and chicken to the Dutch oven (or skillet) and stir until well coated. Add the beer and bring to a boil. Continue to cook for about 3 to 5 minutes. Add chicken stock and all beans.

6. Cook for about 3 to 4 minutes longer until meat registers 165 degrees on a meat thermometer. Serve in large bowls. Sprinkle with fresh chopped parsley.

Tip: Feel free to tweak this recipe to experiment with various beers. The darker the beer you use, the richer the flavor.

CHICKEN BREASTS with BASIL LEMON SAUCE

Serves 4

PREP 6 minutes

COOK 25 minutes

CLEAN 6 minutes

Nothing brings me more joy than a one-skillet chicken dish! Scraping up the crispy, sticky bits from the pan is my favorite part—it's the best way to make a sauce. The lemon, chili and white wine come together so brightly here that you'll find yourself tempted to eat it by the spoonful.

4 medium **CHICKEN BREASTS**, boneless, with skin on

1 teaspoon kosher salt

1 teaspoon freshly ground black pepper

2 tablespoons canola oil

2 medium **SHALLOTS**, minced

½ teaspoon dried chili flakes

½ cup white wine (chardonnay is good)

¾ cup roughly chopped **BASIL**, reserve some for garnish

Juice of 1 lemon

2 tablespoons unsalted butter

Tip: When cooking with wine, cook with what you drink with. Don't get a cheap bottle of wine for cooking; this will affect the flavor. What's one cup out of a decent bottle? And if you're like me, you're likely to have more than one bottle laying around.

Let's Cook!

1. Preheat oven to 400°F. Pat chicken breasts dry, then season the skin well with salt and pepper.

2. In a large ovenproof skillet or Dutch oven, heat canola oil over medium-high heat. Lay chicken breasts skin side down on the hot pan, turning once, until they are browned. This should take about 2 minutes on each side.

3. Place pan in the oven, skin side up, for about 10 to 12 minutes to cook breasts through until meat registers 165 degrees on a meat thermometer. Remove chicken from oven. Take chicken out of the skillet or Dutch oven; set aside and cover with foil.

4. Place the same pan over medium heat. Add shallots and cook for about 3 minutes until softened. Stir in the chili flakes. Add the white wine and let boil for 90 seconds, scraping up any browned bits from the bottom of the pan. (This is known as deglazing.) Add 3 tablespoons of water to thin the sauce slightly, then reduce it by half on a low boil for about 3 minutes.

5. Turn off heat. Add in basil, lemon juice, and butter and stir slowly until everything is incorporated.

6. Place chicken on a platter. Spoon the sauce and shallots over the chicken breasts. Garnish with extra basil shreds.

SIDE DISH SUGGESTIONS: Parceled Lemony Asparagus (p. 171), Parmesan Broccolini (p. 174), Cheesy Polenta (p. 191)

CIDER-BRAISED CHICKEN

Serves 4
PREP 6 minutes
COOK 35 minutes
CLEAN 6 minutes

Cider is in my roots—it is one of the best products in County Tipperary, where I am from. The chicken just soaks up the cider vinegar, and to me, this dish is the perfect blend of tart, savory, and sour. PS: I'm a thigh man! Not only are thighs less expensive than chicken breasts, due to their fat content they are much harder to overcook.

1 tablespoon canola oil
8 **CHICKEN THIGHS**
1 teaspoon kosher salt
1 teaspoon freshly ground black pepper
2 **LEEKS**, thinly sliced
1 tablespoon all-purpose flour
1 cup cider vinegar
2½ cups chicken stock
2 tablespoons unsalted butter
2 tablespoons chopped **PARSLEY**

Let's Cook!

1. Preheat oven to 375°F. Heat canola oil over medium heat in a large Dutch oven.

2. Pat chicken dry, then season with salt and pepper. Add chicken to the pot skin side down. Cook in batches over medium-high heat until browned on all sides, about 4 minutes per batch. This will take about 10 to 12 minutes. When done, set chicken aside on a platter.

3. In the same pot, add leeks, flour, and vinegar, scraping up any brown bits from the bottom of the pan. Bring the sauce to a boil and add chicken stock. Place chicken back into the pot with the juices.

4. Cover the pot and pop it into the oven for 20 minutes.

5. Remove the pot from the oven. Then place chicken on a rimmed baking sheet and broil meat until crispy and a meat thermometer registers 165 degrees, about 1 to 2 minutes on the top shelf of the oven. Leave the oven door open and keep an eye on the chicken when it is broiling, as broiling can burn chicken very fast. Do not walk away!

6. Meanwhile, simmer the sauce in the pot for about 10 minutes over medium heat. Stir in butter until melted. Place chicken on plates, spoon sauce over, garnish with parsley, and serve.

SIDE DISH SUGGESTIONS: Chorizo Roasted Brussels Sprouts (p. 185), Velvety Smooth Mash (p. 165)

☆ Tip: Feel free to use skinless breasts if you prefer for this recipe.

THIRTEEN-SPICE CHICKEN with CRÈME FRAÎCHE

Serves 4
PREP 6 minutes
COOK 20 minutes
CLEAN 6 minutes

The whole philosophy behind this book is to create delicious meals with a minimum of ingredients. This can be tricky when it comes to spices, and that's where Old Bay comes in handy. You get thirteen spices in one ingredient when using Old Bay seasoning. Genius!

4 **CHICKEN BREASTS**, bone in with skin on
2 tablespoons Old Bay seasoning
½ teaspoon salt
½ teaspoon freshly ground black pepper
1 tablespoon unsalted butter
1 tablespoon canola oil
1 cup chicken stock
Juice of 1 lemon
½ cup **CRÈME FRAÎCHE**
2 tablespoons chopped **TARRAGON**, plus whole leaves for sprinkling

Let's Cook!

1. Pat dry chicken breasts.

2. In a Ziploc bag, place chicken breasts with Old Bay seasoning, salt, and pepper. Shake until well coated.

3. In a large skillet over medium-high heat, melt unsalted butter with the canola oil. Cook chicken breasts skin side down until brown, about 3 to 5 minutes.

4. Turn chicken breasts over, then add chicken stock and lemon juice. Let simmer for about 10 to 15 minutes in the liquid until meat registers 165 degrees on a meat thermometer.

5. Remove breasts and set on a platter.

6. Turn heat to low and add crème fraîche and tarragon to the skillet. Gently heat for 2 minutes. Spoon sauce on top of chicken. Sprinkle with extra tarragon leaves and serve.

SIDE DISH SUGGESTIONS: Mexican Street Corn (p. 188), Creamed Brussels Sprouts (p. 186)

ALMOND FIG ROASTED CHICKEN

Serves 4

PREP 3 minutes

COOK 20 minutes

CLEAN 6 minutes

I love when figs are in season. But I'll still eat them when they are not, as I think the dried version is just as sweet. Chicken breasts come alive with figs, and the almonds give the dish some crunch. Close your eyes when you taste it, and you're instantly transported to the Mediterranean.

2 cups port wine

3 tablespoons **GOLDEN RAISINS**

1 cup halved **DRIED FIGS**

½ teaspoon chili powder

½ teaspoon cumin

Juice of 1 lemon

2 tablespoons canola oil

1 teaspoon kosher salt

1 teaspoon freshly ground black pepper

4 large **CHICKEN BREASTS**, skin on

1 cup sliced **ALMONDS**, toasted

Let's Cook!

1. Preheat oven to 400°F.

2. In a large saucepan over medium heat, reduce port with raisins and figs for about 8 to 10 minutes.

3. Meanwhile, in a bowl, mix the chili powder, cumin, lemon juice, oil, salt, and pepper together.

4. Pat dry chicken breasts, then rub lemon-spice mixture all over chicken.

5. Place chicken on a rimmed 36 x 18-inch baking sheet lined with foil. Roast in the oven for 15 to 20 minutes, or until meat registers 165 degrees on a thermometer.

STOP! CLEAN MIXING BOWL.

6. Remove chicken from oven. Spoon sauce over chicken and sprinkle almonds on top. Serve.

SIDE DISH SUGGESTION: Toasted Almond Couscous (p. 192)

Tip: If you have extra time and enjoy the flavor of toasted almonds, toss in a dry skillet for 2 to 3 minutes, continually stirring over medium flame.

FYI: Deglazing is a cooking technique in which you scrape up and dissolve the flavorful brown bits of sautéed meat left in a pan by adding a hot liquid to a hot pan and heating.

A VERY, VERY GARLIC CHICKEN

Serves 4

PREP 6 minutes

COOK 35 minutes

CLEAN 6 minutes

When you read the number of cloves of garlic in this recipe, you will think that this is a misprint or that I am completely nuts. But I promise you, it's neither. This recipe incorporates 40 cloves of garlic, and it's one of the best chicken dishes you'll ever make. The flavor of garlic is prominent, but it mellows tremendously when roasted, so don't panic!

1 whole **CHICKEN**, cut into 10 pieces
2 teaspoons kosher salt
2 teaspoons freshly ground black pepper
4 tablespoons canola oil
40 cloves garlic, peeled, or 20 teaspoons chopped garlic from a jar (½ teaspoon equals 1 clove)
1 tablespoon finely chopped **THYME**
½ cup white wine (I like chardonnay)
1 cup chicken stock
3 tablespoons unsalted butter
Chopped **PARSLEY** for garnish

Let's Cook!

1. Preheat oven to 375°F

2. Pat chicken dry. Season the chicken well with salt and pepper. In a large casserole pot or Dutch oven, heat 2 tablespoons canola oil over medium-high heat. Brown chicken in batches, adding more oil if needed. This will take you about 10 minutes.

3. Add the garlic to the chicken in the pan, then add the thyme. Cover the pan and place it in the oven for about 15 minutes, until all chicken is cooked through and meat registers 165 degrees on a meat thermometer.

4. Remove the chicken to a platter. Cover with foil to keep warm.

5. Bring the pot to a medium-high heat and begin to mash the garlic (if whole) with a potato masher or a fork. Add the wine and deglaze the pan for about 2 minutes.

6. Add the chicken stock and reduce the liquid for about 8 to 10 minutes. Turn off heat, whisk in butter, season to taste, and spoon over chicken. Sprinkle with some parsley and serve.

SIDE DISH SUGGESTION: Parmesan Broccolini (p. 174)

ROAST CHICKEN THIGHS, BACON, AND LENTILS

Serves 4

PREP 6 minutes

COOK 30 minutes

CLEAN 6 minutes

This is a convenient one-pot meal that allows for easy cooking and cleanup. I use thighs because they are hard to overcook. Plus, I feel their flavor lends itself nicely to lentils. I find that lentils, by the way, always benefit from the addition of something salty, so here I add some bacon. This is one of the easiest, most nutritious, filling, and inexpensive meals you'll ever make.

1 tablespoon canola oil

8 **CHICKEN THIGHS**, bone in and skin on

1 teaspoon kosher salt

1 teaspoon freshly ground black pepper

2 **SHALLOTS**, minced

4 slices **BACON**, roughly chopped

2 sprigs **THYME**

2 (14-ounce) cans **GREEN LENTILS**, drained

1 cup **CHERRY TOMATOES**, halved

1½ cups chicken stock

Let's Cook!

1. Preheat oven to 400°F.

2. Heat oil in a large ovenproof Dutch oven or casserole pot over medium-high heat.

3. Pat chicken dry. Season with salt and pepper. In two batches, add the chicken and brown on all sides for about 8 to 10 minutes.

4. Remove chicken from the pan and set aside. Drain fat, reserving 1 tablespoon in the pan.

5. Add shallots, bacon, and thyme to the pan and cook for about 5 minutes, or until the bacon begins to brown. Add the lentils and tomatoes to the pan along with the stock and chicken.

6. Place in the preheated oven and cook for 15 minutes, until meat registers 165 degrees on a thermometer. Serve.

PORK

Cider Pork with Broccolini, page 131

Pork is such a versatile meat, and while many people equate pork with fat, there are actually some cuts out there that are leaner than chicken—pork tenderloin, for example, has less fat than a chicken breast. Pork is also reasonably priced and cooks very quickly. I could go on in praise of pork—it's definitely a Quick Six go-to.

QUICK SIX TIPS FOR PORK

- Pork should be cooked to 145°F., which will result in slightly pink juices.
- Lightly brushing pork with canola oil before cooking helps prevent it from drying out. Pork chops are most apt to dry out, so be careful not to overcook them.
- Do not overcrowd the pan when cooking pork so that it will cook evenly.
- When roasting pork, brown it first on the stovetop to obtain a nice crust before putting in the oven.
- Do not parcook pork and then place it in the refrigerator to be finished later. It must be cooked until done to prevent bacterial growth.
- Remove pork from fridge 30 minutes before cooking to ensure even cooking.

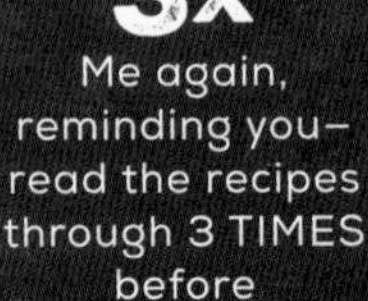

Tools

Aluminum foil

Baking sheet (rimmed, 18" x 13")

Basting brush

Bowls of various sizes

Chef's knife

Cutting board

Dutch oven (large, 5-quart, or casserole, 5-quart)

Grill pan (12-inch) or barbecue grill

Meat thermometer

Paper towels

Parchment paper

Saucepans (small, 1½-quart; and medium, 3-quart)

Skillets (nonstick, 12-inch, ovenproof 12-inch)

Spatula

Spoon (wooden)

Stockpot (4-quart)

Tongs

Whisk

Ziploc bags

PORK CHOP with PORT FIG COMPOTE

Serves 4

PREP 6 minutes
COOK 25 minutes
CLEAN 6 minutes

I love the meaty texture and chew of a good pork chop. Even better, introduce a fruit to the dish and you've got a dream combination. Using fresh figs is optimal, though dried figs are widely available year-round, so that's why I use them here. You can play around with seasonal fruit on this, however. Try subbing in cherries or peaches when they are in season!

- 4 tablespoons canola oil
- 1 tablespoon fresh **THYME** leaves
- 1 tablespoon chopped fresh **ROSEMARY** leaves
- 4 8-ounce **PORK CHOPS**, bone in, about 1 inch thick
- 1½ cups **DRIED FIGS**, halved
- ½ cup red port wine
- Juice of 1 **ORANGE** (about ⅓ cup)

Let's Cook!

1. Divide the canola oil, thyme, and rosemary between two Ziploc bags. Put 2 pork chops in each bag and marinate them in the fridge for at least an hour. Remove from the fridge at least 30 minutes before cooking.

2. Place figs, port, and orange juice in a small saucepan, bring to a simmer, and cook until liquid has reduced by half, about 10 minutes. Set aside.

3. Light a grill or heat a large cast-iron pan until hot, and cook two pork chops at a time until meat registers 145 degrees on a thermometer, about 5 to 7 minutes per side. Set aside to keep warm and repeat with the remaining two. Rest on a plate under tented foil for 5 minutes.

STOP! WHILE MEAT RESTS, CLEAN SKILLET.

4. Transfer to plates and spoon warm compote on top.

FYI: Keeping the bone in helps retain moisture in the meat.

SIDE DISH SUGGESTION: Spicy Sausage Cornbread Stuffing (p. 193)

PORK CURRY IN A HURRY

Serves 4
PREP 6 minutes
COOK 20 minutes
CLEAN 6 minutes

I have been obsessed with curry from a young age and I still can't get enough of it today. This recipe packs a powerful flavor punch smoothed out by Greek yogurt. I love the slight sweetness that the raisins add, too.

- 1½ pounds **PORK LOIN**, cut into 1-inch chunks
- 1 teaspoon kosher salt
- 1 teaspoon fresh ground black pepper
- 3 tablespoons **YELLOW CURRY POWDER**, divided
- 2 tablespoons canola oil
- 1 teaspoon dried chili flakes
- 1 large onion, thinly sliced
- 1 cup whole milk **GREEK YOGURT**
- ½ cup **FROZEN PEAS**, thawed
- 3 tablespoons **RAISINS**
- 2 cups **STEAMED RICE**

Let's Cook!

1. Season pork with salt and pepper.

2. Place pork in a bowl, sprinkle with half the curry powder, and use your hands to massage the curry powder into the meat.

3. Heat canola oil in a large nonstick skillet over medium-high heat. Add chili flakes and cook, stirring, for 30 seconds. Add onion and cook, stirring, until translucent, about 5 minutes. Add the rest of the curry powder and cook for another 2 to 3 minutes, continually stirring. Remove from pan and set aside.

4. Working in two batches, add the pork to the pan and cook until lightly browned all over, about 7 to 10 minutes per batch.

5. Add the first batch of pork and the onion back into the pan with the pork. Add the yogurt and peas and mix thoroughly, using a heatproof spatula.

6. Turn off the heat, add raisins, and stir. Serve over steamed rice.

Tip: Keep an eye on your heat. If it's too high, the yogurt will curdle!

CIDER PORK with BROCCOLINI

Serves 4
PREP 6 minutes
COOK 15 minutes
CLEAN 6 minutes

The county I come from in Ireland, Tipperary, brews the best hard apple cider in the world. It's called Bulmers Irish Cider in Ireland and is exported to the United States as Magners. In this recipe, any apple cider will do if you can't find the best, and the nonalcoholic version works well, too. The vinegar and jelly enhance the apple flavor.

- 4 bone-in **PORK CHOPS**, about ½ inch thick
- 1 teaspoon kosher salt
- 1 teaspoon freshly ground black pepper
- ½ pound **BROCCOLINI**, whole
- 2 tablespoons canola oil
- 2 cloves garlic, crushed
- 2 teaspoons **THYME** leaves
- 1½ cups hard or nonalcoholic **APPLE CIDER**
- ⅓ cup **RASPBERRY OR BLACKBERRY JELLY**
- 3 tablespoons white wine vinegar

Let's Cook!

1. Season pork well with salt and pepper on both sides.

2. Bring a pot of water to a boil. Blanch Broccolini for 3 minutes. Remove and set aside. Season with salt and pepper and keep warm.

3. Heat oil in a nonstick skillet or a griddle pan over medium-high heat. Cook pork for about 4 minutes on each side, or until meat registers 145 degrees on a thermometer. Remove pork from the pan and set aside.

4. Add garlic, thyme, cider, jelly, and vinegar to the pan. Scrape up any brown bits. Let simmer and reduce by half, about 10 minutes.

STOP! SOAK POT USED TO COOK BROCCOLINI.

5. Divide Broccolini and pork chops among 4 plates. Spoon sauce over meat and serve.

SIDE DISH SUGGESTION: Slow Roasted Cherry Tomatoes (p. 178)

BANGERS AND LEEK MASH *with* CRANBERRY COMPOTE

Serves 4

PREP 6 minutes
COOK 45 minutes
CLEAN 6 minutes

Bangers and mash are an institution where I come from—people eat them three or four times a week in Ireland. When I was in junior high school, I remember racing home on my bike at lunchtime. Here's my spin on one of my mom's best dishes. Yukon Gold or baby potatoes fit right into the Quick Six plan, as you don't have to peel them.

2 pounds **YUKON GOLD OR BABY POTATOES**, unpeeled

4 tablespoons olive oil, divided

2 **LEEKS**, roughly chopped, trimmed 1 inch from the white end

¾ cup milk

1 tablespoon kosher salt

1 tablespoon freshly ground black pepper

1 **RED ONION**, peeled and roughly sliced

2 cups **FROZEN CRANBERRIES**

2 sprigs fresh **THYME**

¼ cup balsamic vinegar

8 large **PORK SAUSAGES** (or your favorite type of sausage)

Tip: Frozen cranberries are a great staple to keep in the freezer for when you need to whip up a quick sauce.

RECIPE CONTINUES

RECIPE CONTINUED FROM PAGE 132

Let's Cook!

1. Place potatoes in a large pot. Fill pot with cold water to cover the potatoes. Bring potatoes to a simmer and cook until tender, about 30 minutes (they should be easily pierced with a fork).

2. In another saucepan, sauté onion in 1 tablespoon olive oil for about 5 minutes. Add cranberries, thyme, vinegar, and ¼ cup water. Let simmer for about 10 to 15 minutes, until everything has married together. Remove cranberry onion jam from the pan and set aside in a bowl. Wipe pan and place back on the heat.

STOP! AS CRANBERRY JAM SIMMERS, CLEAN POTATO POT AND FIRST SAUCEPAN.

3. As the potatoes cook, in a saucepan, heat 2 tablespoons olive oil over medium-high heat. Add leeks and cook until softened, 5 to 7 minutes. Add the milk and bring to a simmer. Season with salt and pepper. Turn off heat and set aside.

4. When potatoes are tender, drain them and add hot milk leek mixture. Mash well with a potato masher and mix until smooth. Season to taste, cover with foil, set aside.

5. Add 1 tablespoon olive oil to the pan. Cook sausages over medium-high heat until well browned and firm to the touch, about 5 to 7 minutes, turning all the time. Work in batches, if necessary, to avoid overcrowding.

6. Scoop a mound of mashed potato onto the center of a plate, stick two sausages in the mash, and top with cranberry onion jam to serve.

MUSTARD-CRUSTED PORK with APPLE CABBAGE SLAW

Serves 4–6

PREP 6 minutes
COOK 45 minutes
CLEAN 6 minutes

During Easter time in Ireland, I love to whip up this easy dish for my family. My mom always has three other types of meat in the oven, usually a duck, a goose, and a turkey. Sometimes beef, too. So trying to find the space to make this meat ends up in an annual argument. Every. Single. Time. Just a snippet of Easter with the O'Keeffes.

1 1½-pound **PORK TENDERLOIN**
1 teaspoon kosher salt
1 teaspoon freshly ground black pepper
½ cup **GRAINY MUSTARD**, such as Grey Poupon
2 tablespoons olive oil
1 tablespoon unsalted butter
1 tablespoon white wine vinegar
1 tablespoon light brown sugar
4 cups shredded **CABBAGE**
1 **APPLE**, grated through medium to large holes on grater
2 tablespoons chopped **PARSLEY**

RECIPE CONTINUES

RECIPE CONTINUED FROM PAGE 135

Let's Cook!

1. Preheat oven to 400°F.

2. Pat pork dry and season well with salt and pepper. In a bowl, whisk mustard and olive oil together. Using your hands, rub mixture all over pork tenderloin. Let meat sit until it comes to room temperature, at least 20 to 30 minutes.

3. Place pork on a wire rack on a rimmed 36 x 18-inch baking sheet lined with foil. Place in the oven for 15 minutes. Reduce heat to 350°F. and cook for another 10 minutes or until meat reaches an internal temperature of 145 degrees on a meat thermometer. Remove from oven, set aside, and cover with aluminum foil.

4. In a skillet, heat butter, vinegar, and sugar over low heat until the sugar is dissolved. Then turn up the heat to medium-high, add the cabbage and apple, and cook until the cabbage has wilted somewhat, about 10 minutes. Stir in chopped parsley.

STOP! AS CABBAGE AND APPLE COOK, WIPE DOWN BAKING SHEET, WIRE RACK, AND BOWL.

5. Remove foil from pork and slice.

6. Spread cabbage on a platter, top with pork slices, and serve.

SIDE DISH SUGGESTION: Toasted Almond Couscous (see p. 192)

STICKY RIBS

Serves 4

PREP 6 minutes
COOK 60 minutes
CLEAN 6 minutes

I live for ribs. I get so much satisfaction cooking and eating them, getting every bit of meat off that bone. You'll want to eat every sweet, spicy, tart morsel of this, too. The secret is in the Asian marinade—soy sauce, rice wine vinegar, hoisin sauce, and Chinese five-spice powder make up an unbeatable combination. This one takes a little longer to cook than my other recipes, but it's well worth the wait.

- 2 full racks pork **BABY BACK RIBS**
- 1 1-inch piece of **GINGER**, sliced thin
- 4 cloves garlic, crushed
- 1 cup hoisin sauce
- 1 tablespoon rice wine vinegar
- ¼ cup low-sodium soy sauce
- 1 teaspoon **CHINESE FIVE-SPICE POWDER**
- 3 tablespoons light brown sugar

Let's Cook!

1. Preheat oven to 400°F.

2. Bring a large pot of water to a boil. Add ribs, ginger, and garlic. Bring back to a boil and let simmer for 20 minutes. Turn off heat and let sit for about 5 minutes.

3. In a saucepan, combine hoisin sauce, vinegar, soy sauce, five-spice powder, and brown sugar. Heat until sugar is dissolved and sauce is smooth and thick. Then reduce for about 10 minutes on medium heat. Set aside.

4. Drain ribs and pat dry with some paper towels. Line a 36 x 18-inch rimmed baking sheet with aluminum foil. Place ribs on baking sheet and brush all over with marinade.

5. Place in oven and roast for 30 minutes, basting with a brush every 15 minutes with more marinade.

6. Serve on a platter and spoon extra sauce on top.

SIDE DISH SUGGESTIONS: BBQ Baked Beans (p. 194), Skillet Mac and Cheese (p. 187), Crispy Fingerling Fries (p. 166)

Tip: Buy turkey freshly sliced from the deli counter. It has less sodium, is less expensive, and is better quality than packaged deli meats.

SWEET SPICY BACON, TURKEY, AND BLUE CHEESE SANDWICH

Serves 4
PREP 6 minutes
COOK 25 minutes
CLEAN 6 minutes

I can't have a chapter about pork without addressing a very serious and delicious ingredient—BACON! It's probably my one true addiction. The sugar and spice along with the salty bacon in this recipe makes this sandwich incredibly hard to put down between bites.

8 thick slices **BACON**
¼ cup light brown sugar
1 teaspoon chili powder
½ cup **BLUE CHEESE**, crumbled
½ cup mayonnaise
8 slices country-style **SOURDOUGH BREAD**
8 ounces thinly sliced **TURKEY**
1 cup **ARUGULA**
4 tablespoons unsalted butter, room temperature

Let's Cook!

1. Preheat oven to 400°F.

2. Line a rimmed 36 x 18-inch baking sheet with foil and top with a wire rack. Spread bacon on the rack and sprinkle with brown sugar and chili powder. Bake in the oven until crisp, about 20 minutes.

3. Mix blue cheese and mayo in a bowl together. Set aside.

4. Place 4 slices of bread on the counter and lightly spread with butter. Flip over and spread with blue cheese mayo. Top with bacon, turkey, and arugula.

5. In a large nonstick pan melt 2 tablespoons butter. Put two of the open-face sandwiches on the pan and top with 2 slices of bread. After 2 minutes, using a large heatproof spatula, turn the sandwiches over and cook them on the other side until golden brown. Repeat with remaining two sandwiches.

SIDE DISH SUGGESTION: Crispy Fingerling Fries (p. 166)

STUART'S "PAELLA"

Serves 4
PREP 6 minutes
COOK 30 minutes
CLEAN 4 minutes

Rice is a big part of my diet. It goes with everything and it's so inexpensive. Whether it's Chinese fried rice, jambalaya, or arroz con pollo, if rice is a main component of a dish, then I'm in. I substitute spicy Italian sausage for the traditional Spanish chorizo in my own unique homage to paella.

- 2 tablespoons olive oil
- ¾ pound **SPICY ITALIAN SAUSAGES**, casings removed (I like the spiciest kind)
- 2 cups long-grain rice, uncooked
- 2 (14-ounce) cans chicken broth
- ½ teaspoon dried chili flakes
- ¾ cup **FROZEN PEAS**
- ¾ cup **FROZEN CORN**
- 1 (28-ounce) can diced San Marzano tomatoes, drained
- 1 tablespoon fresh **THYME** leaves
- 1 teaspoon salt
- 1 teaspoon freshly ground black pepper
- 1 tablespoon chopped **PARSLEY**
- 1 lemon, cut into wedges

Let's Cook!

1. Heat olive oil in a large Dutch oven or casserole over medium-high heat. Add sausage and cook until golden brown, about 5 to 7 minutes, breaking sausage up in the pan with a wooden spoon as you cook. Remove sausage and set aside.

2. Add the rice to the pot and stir. Add broth and chili flakes and scrape the bottom of the pan with a wooden spoon. Bring to a boil. Reduce heat to medium and cook for 10 minutes.

3. Add the peas and the corn along with the tomatoes and thyme.

4. Add the cooked sausage, cover the pot, and bring all back to a simmer for another 8 to 10 minutes. Season with salt and pepper and stir.

5. Garnish with chopped parsley and lemon wedges.

6. Place the pot in the middle of the table with a big serving spoon and let people help themselves.

Parmesan Herb-Crusted Beef with Lemony Arugula, page 154

BEEF

While I was growing up in Ireland, meat, especially beef, was a huge part of daily meals, whether breakfast, lunch, or dinner. This chapter presents some of my favorites from over the years.

QUICK SIX TIPS FOR BEEF

- Red wine, port, garlic, freshly ground black pepper, and deep, robust herbs like rosemary and tarragon pair best with beef.
- When grilling beef, go for higher-priced cuts such as filet mignon, sirloin, and New York strip. Tougher, cheaper cuts like chuck and ribs are better suited for braising.
- Always leave beef to rest under tented foil for 5 to 8 minutes after cooking before you cut into it and serve it. This helps the meat retain its juices.
- Always start with a really hot pan or grill to create caramelization on the outside.
- Pay attention to the proper way of slicing certain cuts. Cuts such as skirt steak and hanger steak, for example, should be sliced against the grain.
- Beef should be cooked to 125 degrees for rare, 130–135 degrees for medium rare, 135–140 degrees for medium, 145 degrees for medium well, and 160 degrees for well done.

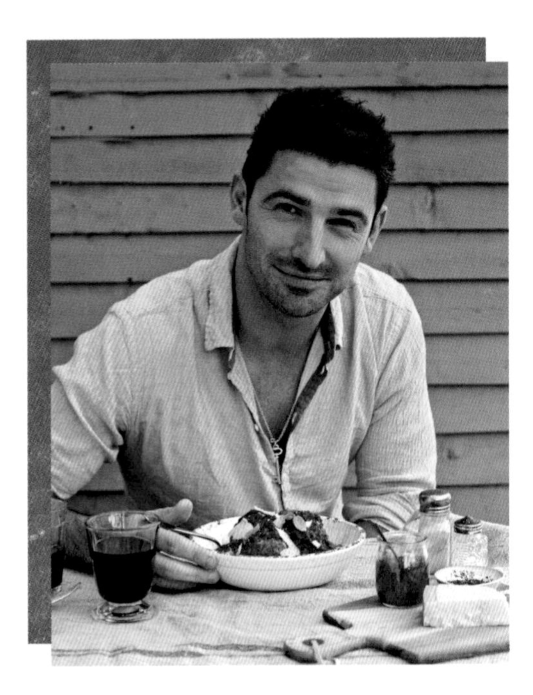

Tools

Aluminum foil

Baking sheet (rimmed, 18″ x 13″)

Bowls of various sizes

Chef's knife

Cutting board

Dutch oven (large, 5-quart, or casserole, 5-quart)

Grill pan (12-inch) or barbecue grill

Meat thermometer

Parchment paper

Skillet (nonstick, 12-inch)

Spatula

Spoon (wooden)

Tongs

Whisk

Ziploc bags

3x
Remember the rule of three: Read recipes through 3 TIMES before you begin cooking!

GARLIC BEEF STIR-FRY

Serves 4

PREP 4 minutes

COOK 20 minutes

CLEAN 6 minutes

My favorite world cuisine? Chinese, hands down. And this is one of my favorite dishes, something I repeatedly order from my local Chinese restaurant up the road (the same one that makes that great dressing mentioned in the salad chapter). I find that Chinese food has many flavor profiles—sweet, spicy, hot, sour, salty—which makes it really hard to grow tired of. This quick dish features garlic and chili, two tastes that go phenomenally well together, especially with beef. The best part of it is, if you buy the steak already sliced, there is literally no prep!

- 2 tablespoons sesame oil or canola oil, divided
- 1 pound **SKIRT STEAK**, cut into ½-inch-thick slices (Have your butcher do this or buy already cut pepper steak strips.)
- 1 tablespoon freshly ground black pepper
- 2 tablespoons **CHILI GARLIC SAUCE**, such as Lee Kum Kee
- ½ pound **GREEN BEANS**, cut in half
- ½ cup **FROZEN PEAS**
- 2 tablespoons **FISH SAUCE**
- ¼ cup beef stock
- 2 cups **STEAMED RICE**

Let's Cook!

1. Add 1 tablespoon sesame oil to a nonstick frying pan or a wok, and heat over medium-high heat.

2. Cook the beef in two batches, stirring until browned, about 7 minutes per batch. Set meat aside.

3. Turn up the heat and add the rest of the oil to the pan. Then add the pepper and chili garlic sauce and cook for about 30 seconds.

4. Put the beef back in the pan along with the green beans, frozen peas, fish sauce, and beef stock.

5. Cook for 4 to 5 minutes until everything is hot and the liquid develops a saucy texture. Serve over steamed rice.

☆ FYI: When stir-frying, it is important to use an oil with a high smoke point, such as canola oil.

PORT-MARINATED SKIRT STEAK with ROASTED GRAPE TOMATOES

Serves 4

PREP 6 minutes

COOK 40 minutes

CLEAN 6 minutes

How to win friends and influence people: cook this steak. Invite people over you want to impress and they will be saluting you by the meal's end. The best part of this recipe is that the marinade is made up of ingredients that you're likely to have in your kitchen already. The sharpness of soy, vinegar, port, and chili permeate the meat, so each bite is packed with flavor.

1½ pounds **SKIRT STEAK**, sinew removed, membrane removed, fat trimmed (Ask your butcher to do this.)

½ cup low-sodium soy sauce

½ cup port wine

½ cup balsamic vinegar

½ teaspoon dried chili flakes

3 **GREEN ONIONS**, roughly chopped

Let's Cook!

1. Preheat oven to 400°F.

2. In a Ziploc bag, combine steak, soy sauce, port, balsamic vinegar, and chili flakes. Marinate for at least 20 minutes.

3. Light a grill or heat up a cast-iron pan over medium-high heat. Remove steak from bag and pour the rest of the marinade into a wide saucepan. Over high heat, reduce marinade for about 5 to 10 minutes, or until thickened.

4. Place steak on grill or cast-iron pan and let cook for 3 to 5 minutes each side. Set aside on a plate under tented foil and let rest for 5 minutes.

STOP! WHILE STEAK RESTS, WIPE DOWN BAKING SHEET AND CLEAN PANS.

5. Slice into ½-inch slices. Drizzle with reduced marinade, sprinkle with green onions, and serve with roasted tomatoes.

RECIPE CONTINUES

RECIPE CONTINUED FROM PAGE 148

ROASTED GRAPE TOMATOES

PREP 3 minutes
COOK 20 minutes
CLEAN 3 minutes

These cherry tomatoes, a spin on the Irish breakfast tomato (see p. 178), are the perfect pairing with this steak, adding just the right pop of sweetness to balance out the char of the meat. The best part—they go well with so many other dishes in this book, too.

- 2 cups **CHERRY TOMATOES**, preferably on the vine
- 2 tablespoons olive oil
- ½ teaspoon kosher salt
- ½ teaspoon freshly ground black pepper

Let's Cook!

1. Preheat oven to 400°F.

2. Place tomatoes on a rimmed 18 x 13-inch baking sheet. Drizzle with olive oil, salt, and pepper.

3. Place in the oven to roast for 15 to 20 minutes, until tomatoes are golden brown and blistered.

THE "LA" CHEESEBURGER

Serves 4

PREP 6 minutes
COOK 15 minutes
CLEAN 6 minutes

We all know that the United States does up the best burger in the world. And from the minute I set foot on American soil, I've made a point to visit a lot of amazing burger joints. This basic recipe, essentially a double cheeseburger, represents the best of the best.

⅓ cup mayonnaise

2 teaspoons **SRIRACHA** chili sauce

4 tablespoons unsalted butter, at room temperature

4 **HAMBURGER BUNS**, sliced in half (If you can find brioche buns, go for it!)

2 pounds **85% LEAN GROUND BEEF CHUCK** made into 8½-inch-thick patties (Get your butcher to do this.)

2 teaspoons kosher salt

2 teaspoons freshly ground black pepper

2 tablespoons canola oil

8 slices **AMERICAN OR EXTRA SHARP CHEDDAR CHEESE**

4 **BUTTER LETTUCE** leaves

4 thin slices **TOMATO**

4 thin slices **RED ONION**

Let's Cook!

1. Combine mayonnaise and sriracha in a bowl. Set aside.

2. Heat two nonstick skillets over medium heat. Butter the hamburger buns on each side and toast them in the skillets until golden brown. This should take about 3 to 4 minutes. Set aside.

3. Season the patties with salt and pepper. Add one tablespoon of canola oil to each skillet over medium-high heat. Cook 4 patties in each skillet for 2 minutes. Now flip the patties over, place a slice of cheese on each patty, and cook for 2 minutes more, or until the cheese starts to melt.

4. Place the bottom parts of the buns on four separate plates, stack 2 burgers on each bun, and top with lettuce, tomato, and onion.

5. Spread the inside tops of the buns with the sriracha mayo, close the burgers, and serve.

SIDE DISH SUGGESTION: Crispy Fingerling Fries (p. 166)

Tip: Make a double batch of sriracha mayo and use as a dipping sauce for the fries.

Tip: Make a double batch of soy ketchup and use as a dipping sauce for the fingerling fries. Or use the sriracha mayonnaise from the preceding recipe as a dipper.

ASIAN BURGER

Serves 4
PREP 6 minutes
COOK 20 minutes
CLEAN 6 minutes

East meets West in this spin on my basic burger recipe. It's all about the soy ketchup!

FOR THE SOY KETCHUP:

¾ cup tomato ketchup
3 tablespoons low-sodium soy sauce
1½ tablespoons hoisin sauce
Juice of 1 lime

FOR THE BURGER PATTIES:

¾ cup rice wine vinegar
1 tablespoon superfine sugar
1 **RED ONION**, ½ minced, ½ sliced into rings
1 pound **85% LEAN GROUND BEEF CHUCK**
1 teaspoon kosher salt
1 teaspoon freshly ground black pepper
¾ cup grated **SHARP CHEDDAR**
1 tablespoon canola oil
4 **SESAME HAMBURGER BUNS**
1 cup **SPINACH** leaves

Let's Cook!

1. In a bowl, combine all ketchup ingredients together. Cover and refrigerate.

2. In a separate bowl, mix vinegar and sugar until sugar is dissolved. Add sliced onion and set aside to pickle.

3. In a large bowl, combine the beef, salt, pepper, cheddar, and minced onion, using your hands.

4. Mix well. Mold 4 patties using your hands; do not press patties too tightly together, as you want moist, juicy burgers.

5. Add the tablespoon of canola oil to a nonstick skillet over medium-high heat. Cook 4 patties 3 to 4 minutes each side. While burgers are cooking, toast the burger buns in a toaster or under the broiler about 30 seconds to 1 minute, until golden.

STOP! WHILE BURGERS COOK, CLEAN BOWLS.

6. Divide spinach among 4 bun bottoms, top with pickled onion and 1 tablespoon of soy ketchup and the bun tops.

SIDE DISH SUGGESTION: Crispy Fingerling Fries (p. 166)

PARMESAN HERB-CRUSTED BEEF with LEMONY ARUGULA

Serves 4
PREP 6 minutes
COOK 15 minutes
CLEAN 6 minutes

Think of this as a richer chicken Parmesan. It has that same great crunchy crust and lovely touch of salty cheese in the flavor. Arugula has a peppery edge that balances it all out, while the lemon dressing perks up every flavor.

FOR STEAKS:

2 cups **BREAD CRUMBS**
¼ cup Parmesan cheese, finely grated
½ cup **PARSLEY**
2 cups all-purpose flour
2 medium eggs
8 **BEEF TENDERLOIN STEAKS** (about 3.5-ounce medallions, ½ inch thick)
1 teaspoon salt
1 teaspoon freshly ground black pepper
4 tablespoons canola oil, divided

FOR ARUGULA SALAD:

4 cups **ARUGULA**
Juice of 1 lemon
3 tablespoons extra virgin olive oil
¼ cup Parmesan cheese

Let's Cook!

1. Combine the bread crumbs, ¼ cup of the Parmesan, and parsley in a bowl.

2. Put the flour in another bowl, and beat eggs in a third bowl. Set the three bowls side by side, flour, eggs, bread crumbs.

3. Season the steaks with salt and pepper. Lightly coat both sides with the flour and dredge steaks first in the egg and then in the bread-crumb mixture. Repeat this with all steaks.

4. Heat a large nonstick skillet over medium-high heat; cook the steaks in a single layer for 2 minutes on each side. Repeat with remaining steaks. Set aside on a plate tented with kitchen foil and let rest for 5 minutes.

5. In a bowl, toss together ingredients for arugula salad.

6. To serve, top each steak with arugula salad.

Tip: Save time and have your butcher cut your steaks into 1/2-inch slices.

QUICK BEEF STEW

Serves 4

PREP 6 minutes
COOK 35 minutes
CLEAN 6 minutes

Guess what—beef stew doesn't have to take several hours to make. This recipe is quick and easy and still offers a long-braised flavor. The secret is using a better grade of meat than you would normally use for a stew. A higher grade means less time cooking. So in order to save time, when you're in the supermarket, reach for the sirloin instead of the chuck.

- 3 tablespoons canola oil, divided
- 2 pounds **BONELESS BEEF SIRLOIN STEAK**, cut into 1-inch cubes (To save time, ask your butcher to slice into cubes.)
- 1 teaspoon kosher salt
- 1 teaspoon freshly ground black pepper
- 1 medium onion, roughly sliced
- 4 cloves garlic, crushed
- 3 **CARROTS**, peeled and cut into ½-inch slices
- 2 cups **BUTTON MUSHROOMS**, halved
- ¾ cup dry red wine, such as a cabernet
- 1 (15-ounce) can cannellini beans, drained
- 1 (28-ounce) can diced San Marzano tomatoes
- 1 tablespoon chopped **CHIVES**

Let's Cook!

1. Heat 2 tablespoons of canola oil in a skillet or Dutch oven over high heat. Season meat with salt and pepper and brown on all sides in small batches. This will take roughly 15 minutes total. Remove meat and set aside.

2. Reduce heat to medium, add onion and garlic, and stir for 3 minutes to soften. Add carrots and cook for another 2 minutes.

3. Add the mushrooms and cook for 4 minutes.

4. Turn the heat up to high, add the wine, and scrape any bits from the bottom of the pan. Reduce the heat to medium and simmer for 4 minutes.

5. Add the cannellini, tomatoes, beef, and beef juices and let simmer for another 3 to 5 minutes.

6. Sprinkle with chives and serve.

SIDE DISH SUGGESTIONS: Parmesan Broccolini (p. 174), Velvety Smooth Mash (p. 165)

ROAST BEEF with BLUE CHEESE CHIVE SAUCE

Serves 4–6

PREP 6 minutes
COOK 40 minutes
CLEAN 6 minutes

My mom would make a blue cheese sauce at Easter and pour it all over a beef roast. I'll tell you a dirty little secret about it: She would use soup packet seasoning and just add cream and some chopped chives and crumbled blue cheese to it. My version eliminates the soup packet and tastes just as great!

- 2 tablespoons canola oil
- 1 tablespoon balsamic vinegar
- 2 teaspoons kosher salt, divided
- 2 teaspoons freshly ground black pepper, divided
- 2 –2½ pounds **BEEF TENDERLOIN** (filet of beef)
- 1½ cups **HEAVY CREAM**
- 1 cup **BLUE CHEESE CRUMBLES**
- 1 tablespoon chopped **CHIVES**

Let's Cook!

1. Preheat oven to 400°F. and heat a large ovenproof skillet over high heat.

2. Meanwhile, mix canola oil, balsamic vinegar, 1 teaspoon salt, and 1 teaspoon pepper together and pour this over the meat. Using your hands, massage the mixture into the meat.

3. Place meat in the hot skillet and sear until brown on all sides. This will take about 5 minutes. Then place in the piping hot oven for 25 minutes for medium rare (140°F).

4. Remove meat from oven and set aside covered with tented foil on a cutting board for at least 10 minutes.

5. While the meat is resting, over high heat, bring the cream to a boil in a small saucepan, about 3 minutes. When boiling point is reached, take off heat, add blue cheese crumbles along with 1 teaspoon salt, 1 teaspoon pepper, and chives. Stir until combined.

6. Slice meat into ½-inch slices and spoon sauce over meat.

SIDE DISH SUGGESTION: Butternut Squash and Carrot Puree (p. 173)

Tip: Always keep a jar of good-quality marinara sauce on hand for a speedy meal.

MEATBALLS

Serves 4–6
PREP 6 minutes
COOK 40 minutes
CLEAN 6 minutes

What a genius invention: balls of meat. You can ladle them on spaghetti. Pile them atop mashed potatoes. Tuck them in a baguette with some melted cheese. Or roll them small and serve them on their own as an appetizer. This recipe turns out soft, juicy rounds with a ton of flavor brought in from sausage meat.

- 1 cup dried **BREAD CRUMBS**
- ¼ cup whole milk
- 2 pounds **85% LEAN GROUND BEEF** (makes 12 meatballs)
- ½ pound **SPICY ITALIAN SAUSAGE MEAT**, casing removed
- 1 cup finely grated Parmesan cheese, plus extra for garnish
- 2 teaspoons dried oregano
- 1 teaspoon dried chili flakes
- 1 teaspoon kosher salt
- 1 teaspoon freshly ground black pepper
- 2 medium eggs, beaten
- 6 tablespoons olive oil
- 1 (26-ounce) jar of a good **MARINARA SAUCE** (I like the San Marzano brand.)

Let's Cook!

1. Preheat oven to 400°F. and line two baking sheets with nonstick parchment paper.

2. In a large mixing bowl, with your hands, combine the bread crumbs, milk, beef, sausage, cheese, oregano, chili flakes, salt, and pepper. Add eggs and oil together and continue mixing, using your hands, until all ingredients are combined.

3. Using a half-cup measure, press the meatball mixture into the cup, then pop out onto your hand and roll into a ball. This will ensure that the meatballs are all the same size. (To make appetizer meatball bites, use a quarter-cup measure instead.)

4. Place meatballs on the baking sheets. Bake for 25 minutes or until slightly browned on the tops.

STOP! AS MEATBALLS BAKE, CLEAN MIXING BOWL AND MIXING CUPS.

5. Meanwhile bring the marinara sauce to a simmer. Place meatballs on a large platter and spoon marinara on top. Garnish with extra Parmesan.

SIDE DISH SUGGESTION: Cheesy Polenta (p. 191)

SIDES

Mexican Street Corn, page 188

BBQ Baked Beans, page 194

Slow Roasted Cherry Tomatoes, page 178

At the end of the day, a good steak is just a good steak and a beautiful piece of fish is merely a beautiful piece of fish. But add the perfect complements to each, and you have the makings of a standout meal. Matching up the right side dishes to the right proteins can take those mains in so many different directions. I make suggestions for side pairings throughout this book, but flip through this chapter with an open mind to mix and match mains and sides to create something truly special in your kitchen, and to make a meal your own.

Tools

- **Aluminum foil**
- **Baking sheet** (rimmed, 18" x 13")
- **Bowls of various sizes**
- **Chef's knife**
- **Cutting board**
- **Dutch oven** (large, 5-quart, or casserole, 5-quart)
- **Food processor**
- **Fork**
- **Parchment paper**
- **Ricer**
- **Saucepans** (small, 1-quart; and medium, 3-quart, ovenproof)
- **Skillet** (nonstick, 12-inch)
- **Spatula** (heatproof)
- **Spoon** (wooden)
- **Stockpot** (4 quart)
- **Tongs**
- **Whisk**

3x
Remember the rule of three: Read recipes through 3 TIMES before you begin cooking!

VELVETY SMOOTH MASH

Serves 4
PREP 6 minutes
COOK 30 minutes
CLEAN 6 minutes

If there's just one thing I do really well, it's make incredible mashed potatoes. My recipe yields a mash that is rich, creamy, and smooth on the palate. My secret weapon: a ricer, which crushes the potato into small bits ready for creaming. If you don't have one, get one now! This dish makes a particularly great partner to pork, beef, and even seafood.

- 4 large **RUSSET POTATOES**, peeled and quartered (To speed up cooking time, cut potatoes even smaller.)
- 4 tablespoons unsalted butter
- 1 cup heavy cream
- 1½ teaspoons kosher salt
- 1 teaspoon freshly ground black pepper
- 1 tablespoon chopped fresh **CHIVES**

Let's Cook!

1. Place the potatoes in a medium-size saucepan. Fill with cold water until they are just covered.

2. Bring to a boil, then reduce the heat and let simmer for 20 minutes, until potatoes are very tender and easily pierced by a fork.

3. Melt butter and cream in a small saucepan over medium heat.

4. Drain potatoes; pass each through a ricer into the same saucepan that potatoes were cooking in. Add in the butter and cream mixture, salt, pepper, and chives and mix using a spatula until potatoes are smooth and creamy.

5. Season to taste and serve.

☆ Tip: Potatoes can be made an hour or so ahead of time. Just place a sheet of aluminum foil on top, pressed into the potatoes to keep them warm, after mashing. (This prevents the potatoes from developing a "skin" on top.)

CRISPY FINGERLING FRIES

Serves 4

PREP 6 minutes

COOK 30 minutes

CLEAN 6 minutes

What's not to love about these baby potatoes? Roasting fingerlings in the oven cuts out time, waste, and mess. You don't have to peel the potatoes, nor do you have to heat up a big pot of splatter-happy oil. All you have to do is rinse them off, slice them lengthwise, and pop them in the oven!

16 **FINGERLING POTATOES**, about three inches long, sliced lengthwise

2 tablespoons olive oil

1 teaspoon kosher salt

¼ cup freshly grated Parmesan cheese

1 tablespoon fresh **THYME** leaves

Let's Cook!

1. Preheat oven to 425°F. Place a rimmed 18 x 13-inch baking sheet in the oven and heat up for 10 minutes.

2. Meanwhile, toss potatoes in a bowl with olive oil and salt. Using your hands, mix well to make sure the potatoes are covered in the salted oil.

3. Remove the piping hot pan from the oven and pour the potatoes onto the tray. They will begin to sear and cook. Shake the tray to ensure there is no overlapping.

4. Roast in the oven for 25 minutes, tossing potatoes halfway through with a heatproof spatula.

5. Remove the tray from the oven and let potatoes cool for 5 minutes.

6. Sprinkle potatoes with Parmesan and thyme leaves. Serve.

Tip: These can also make a great appetizer with my Blender Aioli (p. 168) as a dipping sauce.

BLENDER AIOLI

PREP 2 minutes
COOK 2 minutes
CLEAN 3 minutes

There is nothing like making your own aioli. Think of it as a refined mayonnaise that can give so much flavor to so many different dishes. This sauce really complements seafood well and also makes a great dipping sauce for fries.

4 cloves garlic, peeled
1 cup extra virgin olive oil
2 tablespoons fresh lemon juice
4 egg yolks
½ teaspoon kosher salt
½ teaspoon freshly ground black pepper

Let's Blend!

1. In a food processor, add garlic and ¼ cup of the olive oil and puree for 10 seconds.

2. Add in lemon juice and puree for 5 seconds. Then add one yolk at a time and blend after each addition for about 5 seconds.

3. While the processor is running, add the rest of the olive oil in a slow stream. You will see the mixture begin to resemble mayonnaise. Add in salt and pepper. Refrigerate until needed. This will last 2 days covered.

MINTY PEAS

Serves 4
PREP 2 minutes
COOK 6 minutes
CLEAN 3 minutes

This side is an old favorite of mine from way back. My mom would always make this to go with fish and chips. I really love how the mint makes the flavor of the peas "pop."

- 2 tablespoons olive oil
- 1 **SHALLOT**, minced
- 10 **MINT** leaves
- 1 pound bag **FROZEN PEAS**
- 2 tablespoons unsalted butter
- ½ teaspoon kosher salt
- ½ teaspoon freshly ground black pepper

Let's Cook!

1. In a large saucepan, heat oil over medium heat. Add the shallots, mint and peas. Cook for about 5–7 minutes until steamed through.

2. Using a potato masher, smash peas until they reach desired consistency. (I like mine lumpy.) Serve.

PARCELED LEMONY ASPARAGUS

Serves 4

PREP 4 minutes

COOK 10 minutes

CLEAN 6 minutes

The best way to cook asparagus is to steam it. This way, the nutrients stay in the vegetable. (Boiling, for example, causes those nutrients to escape into the water.) Cooking them in a parcel is a great way to prevent overcooking. Unwrap the package and you'll be left with a steamed spear with some crunch. Try this with some superfast hollandaise (p. 172)—heaven! If you serve the package on a platter, cleanup becomes a breeze.

- 16 **ASPARAGUS SPEARS**, bottoms trimmed
- ½ teaspoon kosher salt
- ½ teaspoon freshly ground black pepper
- 1 small lemon, zested and sliced
- 2 tablespoons unsalted butter
- 1 sprig fresh **THYME**

Let's Cook!

1. Preheat oven to 375°F.

2. Lay out a large sheet (about 16" x 12") of parchment paper and place asparagus in the center with enough parchment surrounding the vegetables so you will be able to close the package up.

3. Sprinkle asparagus with salt, pepper, and zest and top with the lemon slices.

4. Place dots of butter on top along with the fresh thyme.

5. Close all ends of the parchment and fold.

6. Place on a rimmed 18 x 13-inch baking pan and bake in the oven for about 8 to 10 minutes. Remove the parchment and serve.

★ How to Fold a Parcel for Asparagus:
Place asparagus in center of parchment. Fold in two sides of the paper to the center, then smooth down and crease the sides until the paper stays. Do the same for the remaining two sides, smoothing down and creasing until the paper stays.

SUPERFAST HOLLANDAISE

PREP 2 minutes
COOK 5 minutes
CLEAN 3 minutes

The secret to this quick recipe is using a blender. Make this simple sauce to accompany any chicken, beef, or fish dish. Or even pour it over fingerling potatoes!

3 tablespoons champagne or white wine vinegar

3 tablespoons fresh lemon juice

1 tablespoon chopped fresh **DILL**

¾ cup (1½ sticks) unsalted butter

4 egg yolks

¼ teaspoon cayenne pepper

Pinch kosher salt

Let's Cook!

1. In a small saucepan over medium heat, warm the vinegar, lemon juice, and dill together for about a minute.

2. In a separate saucepan, melt the butter slowly over low heat.

3. In a blender or food processor, blend the vinegar mixture for about 20 seconds, until foamy. Add the egg yolks one at a time, quickly pulsing with 3-second intervals.

4. Pour in the melted butter in a stream and keep blending for about 30 more seconds. Add cayenne pepper and salt and blend for 5 more seconds. Serve.

BUTTERNUT SQUASH AND CARROT PUREE

Serves 4

PREP 3 minutes

COOK 20 minutes

CLEAN 3 minutes

For those who have a sweet tooth, your vegetable prayers have been answered. The combination of these two is sweetly transporting. Honey enhances the natural flavors, butter adds a savory balance, and the fresh thyme gives it a homey, herbal edge.

2 pounds frozen **BUTTERNUT SQUASH**, thawed

4 **CARROTS**, peeled and roughly chopped

2 cloves garlic, crushed

1 teaspoon kosher salt

½ teaspoon freshly ground black pepper

1 tablespoon **HONEY**

½ teaspoon **THYME** leaves

2 tablespoons unsalted butter

Let's Cook!

1. In a large pot, combine butternut squash, carrots, garlic, salt, and pepper. Cover the vegetables with cold water and place on high heat. Bring to a boil and simmer until vegetables are tender, about 5 to 7 minutes.

2. Let cool for 5 minutes, then transfer everything into a food processor with honey, thyme, and butter. Puree in batches and return to the saucepan. Stir and keep warm until ready to serve.

PARMESAN BROCCOLINI

Serves 4

PREP 3 minutes

COOK 20 minutes

CLEAN 3 minutes

Unlike most kids, I grew up loving broccoli. My aunt would steam it and melt some salted butter on it. My mother would even mash it with tons of butter. We don't see Broccolini often in Ireland, and when I discovered it in the States, I fell in love with the vegetable all over again. I like to think of Broccolini as the slender, elegant alternative to the thick stalks you usually find. Dress it in cheese, and you have broccoli that is runway ready!

1 pound **BROCCOLINI**

3 tablespoons extra virgin olive oil

½ cup freshly grated Parmesan cheese

Juice of 2 lemons

Let's Cook!

1. Preheat oven to 400°F. and place a rimmed 18 x 13-inch baking sheet in the oven to preheat.

2. Meanwhile, trim the Broccolini at the tough ends and break apart into stalks.

3. Toss the Broccolini with the extra virgin olive oil, massaging the oil into the stalks with your hands.

4. Carefully remove the hot pan from the oven and scatter the Broccolini on the tray. It may start to sizzle, which is fine; we want a little char on the vegetable.

5. Roast in the oven for 10 to 15 minutes until charred and tender, checking halfway through and shaking the pan.

6. Remove from oven. Using a pair of tongs, place on a platter, sprinkle with Parmesan, pour lemon juice over all, and serve.

Tip: Turn the oven on as soon as possible and place the rimmed baking sheet inside before you start the prep. This way, the sheet will be hot and ready when you are.

HONEY GINGER BEETS

Serves 4
PREP 6 minutes
COOK 35 minutes
CLEAN 5 minutes

I like to think of beets as the earth's natural candy. In this dish, ginger, balsamic vinegar, and honey bring out the natural sugars while balancing the minerally flavor of the soil.

1 pound medium-sized **BEETS**, scrubbed, peeled, trimmed, and halved

3 tablespoons unsalted butter

2 tablespoons peeled and chopped **GINGER**

¼ cup balsamic vinegar

2 tablespoons **HONEY**

Let's Cook!

1. Preheat oven to 400°F.

2. Place beets in casserole dish and pour in ½ cup water. Cover with aluminum foil and roast for about 20 to 30 minutes, until a knife is easily inserted into the beets.

3. Remove beets from oven and let sit for 5 minutes to cool.

4. In a skillet, melt butter with ginger, vinegar, and honey. Cook for about 2 minutes.

5. Toss beets in mixture until well coated. Serve warm.

SLOW ROASTED CHERRY TOMATOES

Serves 4
PREP 3 minutes
COOK 10 minutes
CLEAN 3 minutes

We have something known as a "breakfast tomato" back in Ireland—it's an essential part of a full Irish breakfast. My mom would make them all the time, roasting them in the oven along with some sausages, bacon, and mushrooms. The tomatoes on their own go beyond breakfast, however, and their sweet, charred flavor complements so many dishes in this book, particularly meat. When heirlooms are in season, use them. The result is crazy good.

1½ pounds **CHERRY TOMATOES**, on the vine if available
¼ cup extra virgin olive oil
1 teaspoon kosher salt
1 teaspoon freshly ground black pepper
10 **BASIL** leaves, roughly chopped

Let's Cook!

1. Preheat the oven to 400°F. and line a rimmed 18 x 13-inch baking sheet with aluminum foil.

2. Place the tomatoes on the baking sheet and drizzle with oil. Sprinkle with salt and pepper.

3. Place in the oven and roast for 10 minutes, or until the tomatoes are broken down and soft.

4. Remove from the oven and scoop onto a platter, sprinkle with basil, and drizzle any leftover juices on top.

POPCORN CAULIFLOWER NUGGETS

Serves 4–6

PREP 6 minutes
COOK 25 minutes
CLEAN 1 minute

Cauliflower has a bad rep for being bland. This recipe will change the way you think of it, thanks to the cumin and chili that really make these nuggets pop on the palate!

- 2 medium heads **CAULIFLOWER**, broken into popcorn-sized florets
- 3 tablespoons olive oil
- 1½ teaspoons chili powder
- 1 teaspoon ground **CUMIN**
- ½ teaspoon paprika
- 1 teaspoon kosher salt
- ½ teaspoon freshly ground black pepper

Let's Cook!

1. Place a rimmed 26 x 18-inch baking sheet on the center rack in the oven and preheat oven to 425°F.

2. Place all florets in a Ziploc bag along with the rest of the ingredients. Shake and toss well to combine. Let rest for 10 minutes.

3. Remove pan from the oven and empty the bag onto the piping hot baking sheet.

4. Return the pan to the oven for 25 minutes, or until cauliflower is browned all over.

SOY BOK CHOY

Serves 4
PREP 3 minutes
COOK 20 minutes
CLEAN 3 minutes

These greens are healthy, and when dressed up with Asian accents, downright exciting to eat. Soy sauce, fish sauce, sugar, and sesame oil is the unbeatable combination that makes this boy's bok choy pop.

1 tablespoon **SESAME OIL**
3 cloves garlic, chopped
½ pound **BOK CHOY**, leaves pulled apart
2 tablespoons soy sauce
2 tablespoons fish sauce
1 tablespoon brown sugar

Let's Cook!

1. In a large skillet, heat sesame oil over medium-high heat.

2. Add garlic and cook for 30 seconds. Then add bok choy and stir constantly for about 2 minutes.

3. Add soy sauce, fish sauce, and brown sugar and cook a minute longer. Serve.

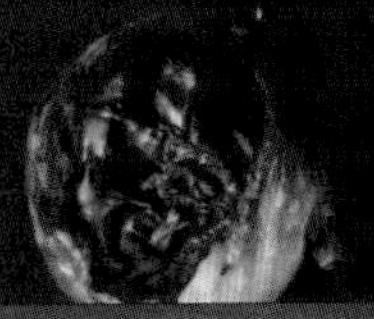

Tip: To cut down on prep time, buy already halved Brussels sprouts at the store.

CHORIZO ROASTED BRUSSELS SPROUTS

Serves 4
PREP 6 minutes
COOK 30 minutes
CLEAN 3 minutes

Hate Brussels sprouts? Try these. You'll eat your words with every last bite. The reason this recipe is so good is that the sprouts are roasted, not boiled! Whoever thought of boiling these veggies in the first place did them a great disservice, as they never taste good boiled. The chorizo in this recipe replaces that green, bitter aftertaste with some meaty pizzazz.

1 pound **BRUSSELS SPROUTS**, halved
3 tablespoons canola oil
2 **CHORIZO SAUSAGES**, halved lengthwise and sliced into ¼-inch pieces
1 **SHALLOT**, minced
4 cloves garlic, minced
1 teaspoon kosher salt
½ teaspoon freshly ground black pepper

Let's Cook!

1. Heat oven to 400°F. Place a rimmed 18 x 13-inch baking sheet into the oven for 10 minutes.

2. Place Brussels sprouts in a bowl and toss with canola oil. Remove hot pan from oven and pour Brussels sprouts onto the tray. They will begin to sear. Do not allow the vegetables to overlap.

3. Roast in the oven for 30 minutes. About halfway through, at the 15-minute mark, remove the baking sheet from the oven. Sprinkle on chopped chorizo, garlic, and shallots and stir on the sheet, using a heatproof spatula.

STOP! CLEAN BOWL.

4. Finish cooking in the oven. Season with salt and pepper. Serve.

CREAMED BRUSSELS SPROUTS

Serves 4–6

PREP 6 minutes

COOK 20 minutes

CLEAN 3 minutes

This is a refreshing spin on creamed vegetables. I thought: if one can enjoy creamed spinach, why not creamed Brussels sprouts? They take wonderfully to the method.

- 1 onion, quartered
- 4 cloves garlic, crushed
- 1 pound **BRUSSELS SPROUTS**, ends trimmed
- 4 tablespoons unsalted butter
- ½ cup chicken or vegetable broth
- 1 cup heavy cream
- 1 teaspoon kosher salt
- 1 teaspoon freshly ground black pepper

Let's Cook!

1. In a food processor, chop onion, then add garlic. Chop again, then add Brussels sprouts and chop in batches. Set aside in a bowl.

2. Heat butter in a large saucepan, then add onion, garlic, and Brussels sprouts mixture. Stir in stock and cook for 7 to 10 minutes over medium heat.

3. Stir in cream, salt, and pepper. Cook for 5 more minutes. Serve.

☆ Tip: Buy Brussels sprouts already shredded to save time.

SKILLET MAC AND CHEESE

Serves 4–6
PREP 6 minutes
COOK 20 minutes
CLEAN 6 minutes

This is a one-pot dish that doesn't even have to go into the oven. The beauty of this side is that it goes straight from the stovetop to the table. Topping it off with bread crumbs adds a terrific crunchy texture to finish.

- 1 pound elbow macaroni
- 3 ounces **CHORIZO SAUSAGE**, rough diced
- 4 tablespoons unsalted butter
- ½ cup all-purpose flour
- 3 cups milk
- 2 teaspoons fresh **THYME**
- 8 ounces **EXTRA SHARP CHEDDAR**, shredded
- 4 ounces Parmesan cheese, grated
- ½ teaspoon kosher salt
- ½ teaspoon freshly ground black pepper
- 1½ cups **ITALIAN SEASONED BREAD CRUMBS**

Let's Cook!

1. Cook pasta according to package directions until al dente.

2. Meanwhile, in a large skillet over medium-high heat, sauté chorizo for 2 to 3 minutes. Remove and set aside.

3. In the same skillet, melt butter over medium heat. Add flour and whisk until a paste forms.

4. Pour milk into the skillet over medium heat while whisking to remove any clumps and until thickened. This will take about 5 minutes.

5. While whisking slowly, add thyme, cheddar, and Parmesan. Season with salt and pepper. Stir until all cheese has melted and it becomes saucy. Add the pasta and chorizo to the cheesy sauce.

6. Top with bread crumbs and serve.

Tip: Make this dish vegetarian-friendly by leaving out the chorizo.

MEXICAN STREET CORN

Serves 4

PREP 4 minutes

COOK 30 minutes

CLEAN 3 minutes

You can find this at any fair or festival in LA. I love the heat of the chili mixed with the sweet of the corn. The creamy mayo and cheese combo lends another layer of textural delight.

- 4 ears fresh **SWEET CORN**, shucked
- ⅓ cup **SOUR CREAM**
- ¼ cup mayonnaise
- ½ cup **CRUMBLED FETA CHEESE**, plus some for garnish
- 1 teaspoon chili powder, plus some for garnish
- ¼ cup chopped **CILANTRO** leaves
- 1 lime, cut into quarters
- ½ teaspoon dried chili flakes, for garnish

Let's Cook!

1. Preheat oven to 375°F.

2. Place corn on the racks of the oven and roast for 25 minutes, or until softened.

3. On a large plate, combine the sour cream, mayonnaise, feta cheese, chili powder, and cilantro.

4. Remove corn from the oven and let cool for 4 to 5 minutes. Roll each ear of corn in the sour cream mixture.

5. Place on a platter, sprinkle with extra feta, chili powder, and chili flakes, and serve with lime wedges.

Toasted Almond
Couscous, page 192

Cheesy Polenta

Spicy Sausage Cornbread
Stuffing, page 193

CHEESY POLENTA

Serves 4
PREP 3 minutes
COOK 10 minutes
CLEAN 3 minutes

This smooth, creamy, cheesy polenta is the definition of comfort. No wonder it's a wintertime staple in the north of Italy. And it's another one of those versatile companions, as delicious alongside meat as it is paired with fish.

- 2 cups water
- 2 cups chicken or vegetable stock
- 1 cup **POLENTA**
- 2 tablespoons extra virgin olive oil
- 1 cup grated Parmesan cheese
- 2 teaspoons chopped fresh **THYME**, **BASIL**, or **CHIVES**

Let's Cook!

1. In a large pot, bring water and stock to a simmer.

2. Add the polenta to the pot in a slow stream, whisking constantly to prevent any lumps. Cook for about 5 to 7 minutes, whisking until it thickens.

3. Stir in extra virgin olive oil, Parmesan cheese, and herbs and serve immediately.

Tip: If your polenta comes out too thick, add some water or stock little by little, until the desired consistency is achieved.

FYI: Be sure to follow the instructions on the polenta package carefully. It may take longer to cook some brands of polenta than others.

TOASTED ALMOND COUSCOUS

Serves 4
PREP 3 minutes
COOK 20 minutes
CLEAN 3 minutes

Couscous is one of the easiest dishes in the world to make. It is also one of the most fun to dress up. This recipe is super simple, with some almonds, garlic, chili, and green onion adding flavor. You can tailor it to your own taste, too. Improvise by tossing in some cherry tomatoes, roasted zucchini, or sautéed eggplant, then fold in some dried raisins, cranberries, or currants for sweetness. You'll find that the pairing possibilities are endless.

- 2 cups **INSTANT COUSCOUS**
- 1 cup boiling water
- 1 cup vegetable or chicken stock
- ½ cup sliced **ALMONDS**
- 1 tablespoon olive oil
- 3 cloves garlic, chopped
- 1 teaspoon dried chili flakes
- 4 tablespoons unsalted butter
- 2 **GREEN ONIONS**, chopped into ¼-inch slices

Let's Cook!

1. Place couscous in a medium-size bowl, then pour boiling water and stock over. Cover and let sit for 3 to 5 minutes until all liquid is absorbed and couscous is tender. (Always read the directions on the package, as different brands can vary.) Fluff with a fork and set aside.

2. Meanwhile, toast the almonds in a dry skillet over medium heat for 2 to 3 minutes. Add to the couscous.

3. In the same skillet, heat olive oil over medium heat. Add garlic and chili flakes along with the butter and cook for 2 minutes.

4. Add garlic chili mixture to the couscous, stir, and season to taste.

5. Scoop onto plates or a platter and sprinkle with the chopped green onion.

SPICY SAUSAGE CORNBREAD STUFFING

Serves 4

PREP 3 minutes
COOK 10 minutes
CLEAN 3 minutes

Cornbread is something that I discovered in the United States. Now I associate it with all things American, especially that most American of holidays, Thanksgiving. Stuff a turkey with some cornbread and watch the faces light up around the table. Same goes for chicken. You can make your own cornbread for this recipe, or you can go the Quick Six route and make this extra easy by using store-bought cornbread muffins. Of course, quick and easy is the way I like to go.

- 1 tablespoon extra virgin olive oil
- 1 onion, diced
- 2 cloves garlic, minced
- 1 teaspoon dried chili flakes
- 2 spicy **ITALIAN SAUSAGES**, casings removed
- 3 cups crumbled **CORNBREAD** (store-bought)
- ½ cup chicken stock
- 1 teaspoon chopped **CHIVES**

Let's Cook!

1. Heat oil in a large skillet over medium heat. Add onion and garlic and cook for 2 minutes to soften up onion.

2. Add chili flakes and sausage and cook for 4 to 6 more minutes, breaking up the sausage with a wooden spoon to ensure it cooks all the way through.

3. Add the cornbread to the pan and stir to combine all ingredients. Add chicken stock and stir. Sprinkle with chives. Serve.

BBQ BAKED BEANS

Serves 4–6

PREP 6 minutes

COOK 20 minutes

CLEAN 5 minutes

I had to learn to make these, as barbecue is one of my favorite things to eat in the States, and barbecue isn't complete without BBQ baked beans. The cannellini beans in this recipe absorb the smoke from the bacon and the sweet brown sugar. Your favorite barbecue sauce will help you whip this up in a flash.

1 tablespoon canola oil

1 teaspoon dried chili flakes

1 onion, finely chopped

2 (15-ounce) cans cannellini beans

1 cup **BARBECUE SAUCE**

¼ cup brown sugar

6 strips **BACON**

Let's Cook!

1. Preheat oven to 400°F.

2. In a large ovenproof saucepan, heat canola oil over medium heat and sauté onion and chili flakes until softened, about 5 minutes.

3. Add beans along with barbecue sauce and brown sugar. Stir to combine.

4. Layer bacon on top of beans.

5. Bake in the oven for 20 minutes. Remove and serve.

GREEN RICE

Serves 4–6

PREP 6 minutes
COOK 25 minutes
CLEAN 4 minutes

Let's be honest—rice can be bland unless you doctor it up with something fabulous. Here's a great shortcut to jazz it up: Toss in your favorite green salsa from a jar. Not only does it give the rice great flavor, but it gives it a nice color, too.

½ tablespoon canola oil
½ onion, chopped
2 cloves garlic, minced
½ teaspoon kosher salt
2 cups chicken broth
½ cup **GREEN SALSA**
1 cup long-grain rice, uncooked
2 tablespoons chopped **CILANTRO**

Let's Cook!

1. In a large saucepan, heat oil over medium-high heat. Add onion, garlic, and salt and cook for 2 minutes.

2. Add broth and salsa. Bring to a boil and then add the rice, continually stirring.

3. Reduce heat and simmer for 20 minutes, or until rice is tender. Turn off heat and let stand for about 5 minutes before serving.

SWEETS

S'mores 2.0, page 207

I actually majored in pastry in culinary school, so there is always room in my day for something sweet. Besides the great finish they provide to a meal, I love desserts because they can often be made ahead of time and assembled quickly. Many people are intimidated by pastry and baking, but there's no need to be! The recipes in this chapter are quite simple to make, even if you are a complete novice. And they are all delicious!

QUICK SIX TIPS FOR DESSERTS

- Keep it simple. You've already cooked a major meal; don't complicate your time in the kitchen with an elaborate dessert.
- If you can prep a dessert ahead of time, do it. You will thank me come serving time!
- There are some great, convenient, premade, timesaving ingredients out there, such as good quality ice cream, frozen pie crusts, and bakery cookies. Don't be afraid to use them!
- Pastry is a bit of a science, so be precise with your measurements. Level off dry cup measurements; be sure to eyeball liquid measurements on the level. Even a slight discrepancy can mess up your dessert.
- Be sure to use dry measuring cups for dry ingredients and liquid measuring cups for liquid ones!

Tools

Aluminum foil

Baking sheet (rimmed, 18″ x 13″)

Baking dish (9 x 5 x 3-inch)

Cake Pan (9-inch)

Dry measuring cups

Ice cream scoop

Liquid measuring cups

Mixing bowls (all sizes)

Ramekins (4, 6-ounce)

Piping Bag (14″ piping bag with #13 star nozzle)

Saucepans (small, 1½-quart; medium, 3-quart; heavy ovenproof)

Skillet (12-inch)

Tongs

Whisk

3x
Me again, reminding you—read the recipes through 3 TIMES before starting!

BRANDIED CHERRIES

Serves 4
PREP 6 minutes
COOK 20 minutes
CLEAN 6 minutes

I got a call to come on the set of the television show *Hart of Dixie* to play myself and prepare cherries jubilee on camera. The thing was, until I got that call, I had no idea what cherries jubilee was! I had to quickly figure it out, and this recipe is the result. The cherries are the true stars here. If they are in season, by all means use fresh ones. Otherwise, frozen cherries work just as well.

- 4 tablespoons unsalted butter
- 1 cup light brown sugar
- 2 pounds **FROZEN CHERRIES**, thawed
- ½ teaspoon kosher salt
- 2 tablespoons **BRANDY**
- Juice of 1 lemon
- 8 scoops good quality **VANILLA ICE CREAM**
- ½ cup crushed **PECANS**

Let's Cook!

1. In a heavy skillet over medium-high heat, combine butter and sugar with 2 tablespoons water and heat until sugar is dissolved, about 5 minutes.

2. Add the cherries and salt. Stir to ensure the cherries are coated with the sugar mixture and cook for about 5 to 7 minutes, or until juices begin to release from the fruit.

3. Turn off the heat. Add the brandy, turn the heat back on to medium, and simmer for about 5 minutes.

4. Add lemon juice and stir.

5. Scoop ice cream into bowls and top with braised cherries and pecans.

RASPBERRY CUSTARD POTS

Serves 4

PREP 6 minutes

COOK 20 minutes

CLEAN 6 minutes

My always baking aunt made custard with everything. When raspberries were plentiful, she would throw a bunch into a custard and bake them. I remember making this with her when I was growing up. It was so delicious, and this recipe is especially for her.

1½ cups fresh or thawed frozen **RASPBERRIES**, plus extra for garnish

3 medium egg yolks

2 medium egg whites

1½ cups heavy cream

½ cup superfine sugar

2 teaspoons vanilla extract

¼ cup **CRÈME FRAÎCHE**

Let's Cook!

1. Preheat the oven to 350°F. Lightly grease four 6-ounce ramekins with cooking spray.

2. Place 3 raspberries in the bottom of each ramekin.

3. Whisk egg yolks, egg whites, cream, sugar, and vanilla together until smooth.

4. Divide the egg mixture and then most of the rest of the raspberries among the ramekins, remembering to reserve some for garnish.

5. Bake in the oven for about 20 minutes until the custard is just firm.

6. Remove from oven and let sit for about 5 minutes before serving. Add a dollop of crème fraîche on top and sprinkle with one or two extra berries.

Tip: You can sub in any berry or fruit for the same tasty result!

A BIG DELICIOUS SWEET CHOCOLATE MESS

Serves 4
PREP 3 minutes
COOK 10 minutes
CLEAN 5 minutes

This is a spin on the classic Eton mess, which is a popular dessert where I'm from. A mixture of cream, meringue, and fruit, it's painless to prepare. Berries are my choice of fruit, but feel free to change this up to your own whims and taste.

2 cups heavy cream, divided

2 ounces **BITTERSWEET CHOCOLATE** (60% cacao)

4 cups lightly crushed store-bought **MERINGUES**

1 cup **STRAWBERRIES**, rinsed, stems removed, and halved

1 cup **RASPBERRIES**, rinsed

½ cup shelled unsalted **PISTACHIOS**, roughly chopped

Let's Cook!

1. Put the chocolate in a heatproof bowl. In a heavy saucepan, heat ½ cup of the cream on low until a light simmer. Pour cream over chocolate. Stir together, set aside, and let cool for 5 minutes.

2. Whip remaining 1½ cups cream to form soft peaks. Set aside.

3. Place ½ cup crushed meringues into each of 4 serving bowls or small mason jars or martini glasses.

4. Sprinkle with the berries of choice, then drizzle with chocolate. Top each with remaining meringue, berries, chocolate sauce, and finally ½ cup whipped cream.

5. Top with chopped pistachios.

S'MORES 2.0

Serves 4

PREP 3 minutes
COOK 10 minutes
CLEAN 2 minutes

S'mores are indeed yummy. But how many of us have a campfire at the ready? This recipe is genius because you don't need to build a fire. You don't even need to have a grill for it. The first time I made these for my next-door neighbors, they became hooked. Suddenly, it seems they always have the three ingredients necessary to make them on hand! All it takes is chocolate chip cookies, some good quality chocolate squares, some marshmallows, and your broiler.

8 large **CHOCOLATE CHIP COOKIES**
8 ounces of good quality **CHOCOLATE** (such as Ghirardelli), roughly chopped
12 **MARSHMALLOWS**

Let's Cook!

1. Set the broiler to medium in your oven. Move the oven rack one from the top.

2. On a lined baking sheet, lay out 4 cookies (flat part of cookie facing up). Place a sprinkling of chocolate on each, then three marshmallows on top.

3. Place the baking sheet in the oven and cook until the marshmallows begin to become golden. Check on them every 30 seconds, as they can burn pretty fast.

4. Remove from oven and press a second cookie on top. Serve with a big glass of cold milk.

Tip: Do not walk away from the broiler when cooking! Check on the s'mores about every 30 seconds so they don't burn. Cooking will take about a minute and a half total.

MOLASSES VANILLA ICE CREAM SANDWICHES

Serves 4

PREP 3 minutes
COOK 12 minutes
CLEAN 2 minutes

Molasses cookies and vanilla ice cream—this may not be the world's most groundbreaking combination, but it's one of those simple pleasures I crave over and over again. Biting into one of these sandwiches makes me happy every time.

1½ cups all-purpose flour
1½ teaspoons baking soda
1 teaspoon ground cinnamon
½ teaspoon ground **GINGER**
½ teaspoon kosher salt
1 medium egg
6 tablespoons unsalted butter, at room temperature
⅓ cup granulated sugar
¼ cup **MOLASSES**
2 tablespoons dark brown sugar
1 pint good quality **VANILLA ICE CREAM**

Let's Cook!

1. Preheat oven to 375°F. Line a baking sheet with parchment paper. Place rack in the middle of the oven.

2. In a large bowl, whisk together flour, baking soda, cinnamon, ginger, and salt and set aside.

3. In a separate bowl, whisk together egg, butter, sugar, molasses, and brown sugar.

4. Stir dry ingredients into the wet ingredients until well combined.

5. Sprinkle some granulated sugar in a bowl. Roll ¼ cup of cookie dough in your hand to form a ball, toss in sugar to coat, and shape to form a disk of about 2½ inches in diameter. Place on baking sheet, 1 inch apart.

6. Bake cookies for 10 to 12 minutes, until cracks form on the tops. They will be soft but will harden as they cool. Place a scoop of ice cream between two cookies and serve.

Tip: Feel free to substitute brioche or challah for the croissants.

BLACK AND WHITE CROISSANT BREAD PUDDING

Serves 4–6

PREP 6 minutes
COOK 20 minutes
CLEAN 6 minutes

This dessert is a big hit at parties in the Hollywood Hills, especially in the cooler months. It's probably one of my most deceptive desserts—everyone thinks it's complex to prepare, but it's one of the simplest desserts in my repertoire. When the bread pudding is firm to the touch, you know it's done.

1 tablespoon unsalted butter, at room temperature

3 medium eggs, plus 3 additional yolks

1 cup heavy cream

1 cup whole milk

½ cup plus 1 tablespoon light brown sugar

2 teaspoons vanilla extract

5 one-day-old **CROISSANTS**

5 ounces **BITTERSWEET CHOCOLATE CHIPS** (70% cacao)

5 ounces **WHITE CHOCOLATE CHIPS**

1 cup **CRÈME FRAÎCHE** or **WHIPPED CREAM**

Let's Cook!

1. Preheat oven to 375°F. Butter the bottom of a 9 x 5 x 3-inch baking dish with your hands.

2. In a large bowl, whisk whole eggs and yolks, cream, and milk with the ½ cup brown sugar and vanilla extract.

3. Tear up croissants and mix with egg mixture until well combined.

4. Spoon half of the egg croissant mixture into the baking dish, sprinkle with dark and white chocolate chips, top with more egg croissant mixture, and finish with remaining chocolate. Sprinkle with 1 tablespoon brown sugar.

5. Place the dish on a rimmed baking sheet and bake in the oven for 15 to 20 minutes, or until firm to the touch.

6. Remove from oven. Serve with a dollop of crème fraîche or whipped cream.

Tip: Ask your baker for marked-down croissants at the end of the day.

SWEET BERRIES "YORKSHIRE PUDDING"

Serves 4
PREP 6 minutes
COOK 20 minutes
CLEAN 6 minutes

Even though in Ireland Yorkshire pudding is used as a savory sopping mop for gravy from a roast, I started to imagine, what if that gravy were sweet? What if I added a little sugar to my dough and berries as the garnish? This lovely puffy delicious dessert is the result of that doughy daydream.

¾ cup all-purpose flour
3 tablespoons superfine sugar
3 medium eggs
¾ cup milk
2 teaspoons vanilla extract
4 tablespoons unsalted butter
1 cup **MIXED BERRIES** (blueberries, strawberries, blackberries, raspberries)
Powdered sugar for garnish

Let's Cook!

1. Preheat oven to 400°F. Place a heavy ovenproof saucepan in the oven (cast iron is good for this). Leave it in for about 10 to 15 minutes to heat up.

2. Meanwhile, whisk flour and sugar together in a bowl. Make a well in the center.

3. In a separate bowl, whisk eggs, milk, and vanilla together.

4. Pour wet ingredients into the well of the dry ingredients and whisk until smooth.

5. Carefully remove the piping hot pan from the oven. Place butter in pan and swirl around until melted. Pour in batter and return to the oven. Bake for 20 minutes or until the cake puffs up and is browned.

6. Place pan in the middle of the table, covering the handle with a towel. Top with a few scoops of ice cream and fruit. Sprinkle powdered sugar on if desired. Serve.

CHURROS

Makes 15

PREP 6 minutes
COOK 30 minutes
CLEAN 6 minutes

When I went to my first theme park in England at seven years old, I ate my first doughnut, then promptly died and went to heaven. I was especially impressed by the fluffiness of those particular doughnuts. Flash-forward to my moving to LA. I rediscovered that same bliss in this amazing traditional Mexican dessert. This recipe may be a bit more complicated than the other desserts, but once you get it down, the technique never leaves you.

1 cup water
½ cup (1 stick) unsalted butter, cut into quarters
1 cup all-purpose flour
3 medium eggs
1 cup sugar
2 tablespoons ground cinnamon
Vegetable oil, for frying
For dipping: a good **CHOCOLATE** or **CARAMEL SAUCE** or both

Let's Fry!

1. Heat 4 inches oil to 370°F. (using a kitchen thermometer) in a wide 3½- to 4-quart heavy pot over high heat. IMPORTANT: Never leave heating oil unattended in the kitchen.

2. While the oil is heating, bring water and butter to a simmer in a saucepan. Remove from heat, and stirring fast, add in the flour until it becomes thickened into a dough. Add in one egg at a time, continuously stirring.

3. Spoon the dough into a 14-inch piping bag fitted with a No. 13 star nozzle.

STOP! WHILE WAITING FOR OIL TO FINISH HEATING, CLEAN SAUCEPAN.

4. Mix the sugar and cinnamon together on a large plate. Set aside.

5. Working in batches, pipe no more than five 4-inch pieces of dough into the oil at one time, using a sharp knife to release dough from the nozzle. Let cook until browned all over.

6. Using a pair of tongs, remove all pieces from the oil and toss in the sugar mixture. Serve with your favorite dipping sauce.

DERRY'S GUINNESS CAKE

Serves 4
PREP 5 minutes
COOK 90 minutes
CLEAN 5 minutes

When I was growing up, my Aunt Derry would make this cake every single week without fail. I adored this cake with a light spread of butter on each slice and a cup of tea. Yes, the baking time is a bit long, but the prep and cleanup time are short and simple.

- 1 cup unsalted butter, plus more for greasing
- 1½ cups brown sugar
- 8 ounces **GUINNESS STOUT**
- Zest of 1 **ORANGE**, grated
- 1 cup **GOLDEN RAISINS**
- 4 cups white flour
- ½ teaspoon baking soda
- 3 eggs, lightly beaten

Let's Cook!

1. Preheat the oven to 350°F. Grease a deep, 9-inch cake pan with butter.

2. Place the butter and sugar in a small saucepan and melt the butter over low heat, stirring to dissolve the sugar.

3. Stir in the stout. Add the orange zest and golden raisins. Turn up the heat to high and bring to a boil, stirring frequently, for 3 minutes. Remove from the heat and set aside to cool.

4. Sift the flour and baking soda together into a large bowl. When the Guinness mixture has cooled to lukewarm, stir it into the flour mixture. Slowly add the eggs, mixing well.

5. Spoon the batter into the pan, and bake for 1½ hours or until a toothpick inserted in the middle of the cake comes out clean.

6. Let cake cool before serving.

CHOCOLATE ESPRESSO "TIRAMISU"

Serves 4

PREP 6 minutes

COOK 20 minutes

CLEAN 6 minutes

Thought tiramisu was time-consuming to make? Think again. This recipe uses some shortcuts while retaining the flavors of chocolate, coffee, cake, and cream.

- 1 cup heavy cream, divided
- ½ cup whole milk
- 8 ounces **DARK CHOCOLATE CHIPS** (60% cacao)
- ½ cup brown sugar
- 2 cups brewed strong dark roast **COFFEE**, at room temperature
- 2 cups **MASCARPONE CHEESE**
- 1 teaspoon vanilla extract
- One loaf **POUND CAKE**
- Drizzle of **CHOCOLATE SAUCE**

Let's Cook!

1. In a saucepan, bring ½ cup of the cream and the milk to a simmer. Turn off heat, add chocolate, and stir until chocolate has completely melted. Pour into a bowl and set aside.

STOP! RINSE AND CLEAN SAUCEPAN.

2. In the same saucepan, over medium-high heat, dissolve sugar in coffee for about 3 minutes. Turn off the heat and set aside to cool.

3. In a bowl, whisk together the mascarpone, remaining ½ cup cream, and vanilla. Set aside in the refrigerator for up to 20 minutes to thicken.

4. Place one slice of pound cake in the center of a plate and spoon some coffee mixture on top of the cake. Top with one tablespoon of the mascarpone mixture. Place another slice on top, add more mascarpone, and drizzle with chocolate sauce.

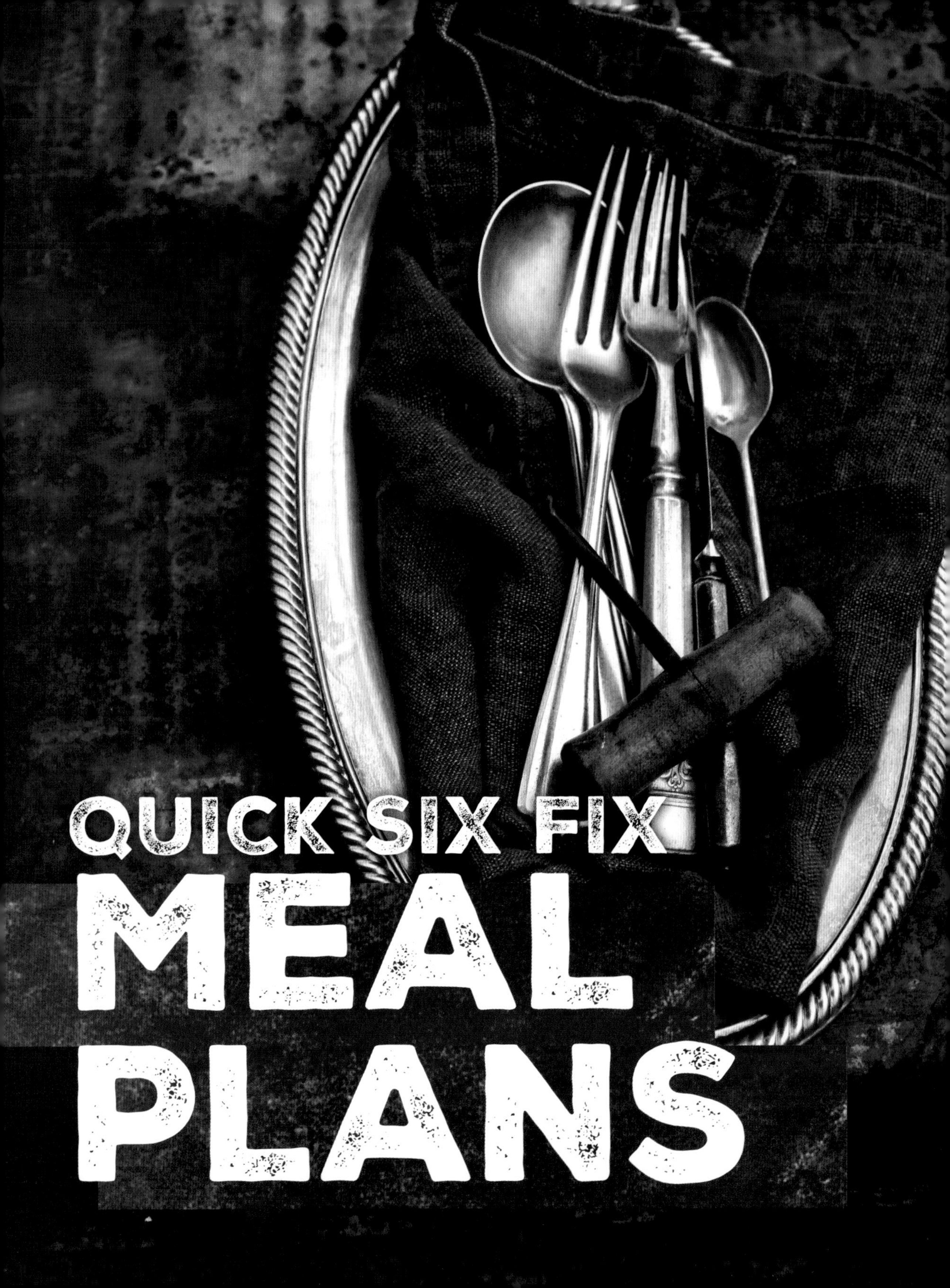
QUICK SIX FIX
MEAL
PLANS

SAMPLE QUICK SIX SIX-DAY MEAL PLANS

In keeping with the Quick Six Fix philosophy, I've put together a sample meal plan for a 6-day week. (Take the seventh day off—eat out, order in, do whatever you like, but even a cook deserves a rest!)

This meal plan is a good example of one that shows balance and variety. It makes use of leftovers, uses several items on the shopping list more than once, and there are not too many perishables. Many of the dishes are complete meals, so no need to fuss over side dishes for some. Two desserts provide ample reward for the week.

Day One

BREAKFAST:
Lemon Chili Avocado Toast

LUNCH:
Tex Mex Salad with Lime Avocado Dressing

DINNER:
Chicken Breasts with Basil Lemon Sauce

SIDE DISH SUGGESTIONS:
Parceled Lemony Asparagus
Cheesy Polenta

Day Two

BREAKFAST:
Blueberry Kick Smoothie

LUNCH:
Asian Burger with Fingerling Fries

DINNER:
Butternut Squash and Coconut Soup

DESSERT:
S'mores 2.0

Day Three

BREAKFAST:
Speedy Gonzalez Eggs

LUNCH:
Asian Chicken and Mint Salad with Asian Dressing from up the Street

DINNER:
Crispy Salmon with Pistachio Basil Butter

SIDE SUGGESTIONS:
Minty Peas or Parceled Lemony Asparagus

Day Four

BREAKFAST:
School-Morning Oatmeal

LUNCH:
Sweet Spicy Bacon, Turkey, and Blue Cheese Sandwich

DINNER:
Fast Bacon and Shrimp Tagliatelle

Day Five

BREAKFAST:
Poached Eggs, Goat Cheese and Spinach on Toast

LUNCH:
Kale, Fingerling Potato and Bacon Salad with Super Citrus Dressing or Lime Avocado Dressing

DINNER:
Ten-minute Coconut Shrimp Curry

Day Six

BREAKFAST:
A Manhattan Breakfast

LUNCH:
My Mother's Chicken Noodle Soup

DINNER:
Angel Hair with Lemon, Kale and Pecans

DESSERT:
Raspberry Custard Pots

SHOPPING LIST

(Note that pantry items are not included. Check that you have ample pantry items for the week.)

FRUITS AND VEGETABLES

16 asparagus spears
3 ripe avocados
1 medium orange
1 medium tomato
3–4 cups cherry tomatoes (about 30–35)
7 cups spinach leaves (a little over a pound)
½ pound baby spinach
1 head romaine lettuce
1 cup arugula
1 pound kale greens
1 large head white cabbage
1 cucumber
4 green onions
2 red onions
3 large shallots
4 medium carrots
1 4-inch piece of ginger
1 jalapeno
1 red bell pepper
½ pound baby potatoes
2 celery stalks
2 cups button mushrooms

HERBS

One bunch fresh chives
One bunch fresh parsley
One bunch basil leaves
One bunch cilantro leaves
One bunch mint leaves
4 sprigs fresh thyme

BREAD/GRAINS

4 slices pumpernickel bread
8 slices whole wheat bread
12 slices sourdough bread
1 package instant oatmeal
4 sesame hamburger buns
1 18-ounce box of old-fashioned oats
1 cup polenta

DAIRY

4 ounces goat cheese
4 tablespoons cream cheese
2 cups Greek yogurt
¾ cup sour cream
¾ cup grated sharp cheddar
1 package blue cheese crumbles
2 cups mascarpone cheese

FISH

4 6-ounce salmon fillets
8 ounces smoked salmon
1½ pounds uncooked medium shrimp (about 60–70)

MEAT

3 two-pound, pre-cooked rotisserie chickens
18 slices thick-cut bacon
1 pound 85% lean ground beef chuck
4 medium chicken breasts, boneless with skin on
8 ounces thinly sliced turkey (from deli)

NUTS

¾ cup sliced almonds
¾ cup chopped walnuts
¼ cup shelled pistachios
½ cup pecans

FROZEN

2 cups frozen blueberries
2 pounds frozen, cubed butternut squash

BAKING

8 ounces dark chocolate chips (60% cacao)
Chocolate sauce
4 squares of good quality chocolate (such as Ghirardelli)
Almond extract

OTHER

Medium bag of tortilla chips
Small bag of marshmallows
One loaf pound cake
8 chocolate chip cookies
3 tablespoons Thai red curry paste
4 teaspoons honey
1½ tablespoons toasted sesame oil
4 tablespoons strawberry jam

PANTRY LIST

Check your pantry to make sure you have more than enough:

Lemon
Lime
Sea salt
Pepper
Dried Chili flakes
Unsalted butter
Eggs
Black beans
Coconut milk
Canola oil
Whole milk
Heavy cream
Onions
Sugar
Distilled white vinegar
Extra virgin olive oil
Sesame seeds
Garlic
Peanut oil
Soy sauce
Balsamic vinegar
Dijon mustard
Ketchup
Hoisin sauce
Rice wine vinegar
Light brown sugar
Chili powder
Mayonnaise
Chicken stock
Pasta
Rice
Parmesan
Dark roast coffee
Vanilla extract
White wine

A few pointers when planning for a week of eating:

1. Check the weather forecast at the beginning of the week and plan accordingly. You don't want to plan barbecues for a week that says rain, for example. Or if a cold spell is coming, it might be a good week for soups and stews.

2. Always make a complete shopping list at the beginning of the week to save yourself the time of running back and forth to the market. While making your list, check your pantry to make sure you have enough Quick Six Fix pantry items for the week.

3. Take a look at your week and make sure your proteins, vegetables, starches and sweets have good variety. Also: keep in mind that there's no need to have dessert every night!

4. Balance each day according to your lifestyle. For example, if I know that I usually have an early meeting on Monday mornings, I don't spend too much time on breakfast—so Monday is a good choice for a quick smoothie day for me. On the weekends, I know I'll likely be outdoors and active, so I'll plan heartier breakfasts. Also, try and trade off heartier and lighter fare for the rest of the day. If I'm having a salad for lunch, for example, it's likely I'll crave a heartier dinner.

5. Cook the most perishable items first! Don't leave that gorgeous salmon until the very end of the week. Enjoy it fresh.

6. Incorporate your leftovers into other meals during the week. Or make extra. That chicken you made? Save the rest for a salad. The leftover pasta or rice? Think about tossing it in a soup.

QUICK SIX THEMED MENUS

Not every meal is an occasion, but there are those dishes that taste best during certain times. Whether celebrating a holiday, having a dinner party or merely catering to the kids, here are 6 top themes with 6 great suggestions.

Holidays

Roast Beef with Blue Cheese Chive Sauce

Mustard-Crusted Pork with Apple Cabbage Slaw

Almond Fig Roasted Chicken

Crispy Salmon with Pistachio Basil Butter

Simple Arugula Salad

Brandied Cherries

Outdoor

Port-Marinated Skirt Steak with Roasted Grape Tomatoes

Sticky Ribs

Asian Burger

Mexican Street Corn

Steakhouse Salad

S'mores 2.0

Cold Weather

White Bean Chicken Soup

Pea and Ham Soup

Speedy Cioppino

Quick Beef Stew

Three-Bean Beer Chicken

Chocolate Espresso Tiramisu

Dinner Party

Pork Chop with Port Fig Compote

Moules Frites

Package-Parceled Cod

Curried Chicken Dinner

Garlic Beef Stir-Fry

Easy Chicken Risotto

Picnic

Simple Bread Salad

Mediterranean Tomato Pasta

Roast Chicken Thighs, Bacon and Lentils

Jumbo Shrimp Roll with Spicy Chile Butter

Sweet Spicy Bacon, Turkey, and Blue Cheese Sandwich

Sweet Berries "Yorkshire Pudding"

Kid Friendly

Stuart's Irish Yankee Mac and Cheese

The "LA" Cheeseburger

Meatballs

Buffalo Chicken Wings, Maytag Blue Cheese Dipping Sauce

Penne with Tomatoes and Bacon

Churros

Meatballs, page 161

Acknowledgments Stuart would like to thank: my parents for their constant support, especially in my moving to the United States, becoming a chef, and following my dreams—and specifically my mom, for getting me in the kitchen when I was a kid, and my dad, who has been such a great cheerleader for my whole journey; my aunt, for showing me how to be a great baker; my two brothers, Graham and Frank, and my sister Grainne, who collectively supported me along the way; my best friend and manager, Jason Pinyan, for helping me find my way through Hollywood and making this a reality for me; Amy Breshears, Craig Gordon, and Alison Roades-Brown, for being my greatest friends and watching all this happening; my food stylist, Sharon Hearne-Smith; Joanne Murphy, for her amazing photography; Grace Campbell, for props; Jean Kwolek, for her support; Katherine Latshaw, my agent at Folio; my editors Becca Hunt, for acquiring the book, and Deb Brody, for shepherding it through; my amazing coauthor, Kathleen Squires, for keeping me on track and making this process fun; my two dogs, Jack and Bo, for putting a smile on my face at the end of each day.

Sticky Ribs, page 138

ABOUT THE AUTHOR

CHEF STUART O'KEEFFE grew up in Nenagh, Ireland, where he developed a passion for cooking by watching

his mother put together nutritious meals fresh from the farmers' markets. He studied cooking at the Dublin Institute of Technology and graduated with a B.A. in culinary arts. Shortly after, O'Keeffe traveled through Europe, moved to France, and learned high-end French cooking in Bordeaux by working in a small restaurant. At twenty-two, O'Keeffe moved to Napa Valley and was a chef at the Michelin-starred Meadowood in St. Helena. By 2004, he had moved to Los Angeles and was cooking for A-list celebrities, private clients, and parties in Hollywood. Stuart appears frequently on television, including the primetime NBC program *Food Fighters*, Food Network's *Private Chefs of Beverly Hills*, and his own cooking show in Ireland, *Stuart's Kitchen*. Chef Stuart is also known to Americans as a featured chef on OWN's Daytime Emmy–winning *Home Made Simple*. He has also made an iPad and iPhone app of *Stuart's Kitchen*, and was one of the first celebrity chef contributors to Apple's iPad App of the Week, Appetites. He is also the star of the AOL web series *Kitchen Daily 101*.

Chef Stuart's signature easy, quick, hearty, but healthy recipes drive his Quick Six Fix philosophy. He was the North American chef for Tupperware brands, and was the global spokesman for Asiana Airlines's "Fly with Color" campaign. Stuart lives in Los Angeles with his two Westies, Jack and Bo.

Keep up to date with Stuart at **CHEFSTUART.COM**, **@CHEFSTUART_** on Twitter and **CHEFSTUARTOKEEFFE** on Instagram, and **CHEF STUART O'KEEFFE** on Facebook and YouTube.

INDEX

Note: Page references in *Italics* indicate photographs.

S

T

V

W

Y